THE GIRL WITH THE STURGEON TATTOO

THE GIRL WITH THE STURGEON TATTOO

A PARODY **LARS ARFFSSEN**

 St. Martin's Griffin ≈ New York

För Jakob and Milö

www.stmartins.com

Library of Congress Cataloging-in-Publication Data

Arffssen, Lars.
    The girl with the sturgeon tattoo : a parody / Lars Arffssen.—1st ed.
        p.   cm.
    ISBN 978-0-312-61050-0
    1. Murder—Investigation—Sweden—Fiction.   2. Journalists—Sweden—Fiction.
I. Title.
    PS3604.O928G57   2011
    813'.6—dc22

                                                            2011019838

First Edition: September 2011

10 9 8 7 6 5 4 3 2 1

ONE

FREDAG, JANUARI 7

63.7% of crimes of bestiality go unreported by their victims.
—SWEDISH TASK FORCE ON VICTIMS OF BESTIALITY, 2009

They lay naked on the ergonomic Dux mattress, limbs entwined like two meatballs. It was three in the afternoon, and already pitch-dark.

"Was it good for you, too?" Professor Dr. Sven Svenssen asked, turning on his side to face his new lover.

The girl nodded, then snapped him across the nose with her female condom. "That," she said, "was for all the women you've anally raped."

Dazed, the famous scientist rubbed his nostril. "What on earth?"

"And that," she said, fiercely elbowing him in the liver, "is for touching your little sister in the bathtub."

"Are you crazy? I don't have a little sister." Svenssen swore the three-fingered oath of the Nykterhetsrörelsens Scoutförbund, the Swedish scouting organization he belonged to as a youth, when he learned how to survive on elk scat and shriveled lingonberries.

"And this," she said, brutally stabbing her iPod charger into his belly button, "is for tying your grandmother to the roof rack of your Volvo."

"She was already frozen solid!" said Svenssen.

When the throbbing subsided, he eyed his new lover cautiously. She was still glowering at him, but her lips were quivering. He reached out and gave her death-black hair a tentative touch, where the red roots were starting to show. She acquiesced, breathing quietly.

"You've obviously had some unpleasant experiences with men," he said gently.

The girl shrugged and then spat across the room. She wasn't very ladylike. Nor very talkative. Life evidently had made her hard, Svenssen reflected. But he wasn't going to pry.

She lit a cigarette and pulled the sheet across her breasts. It occurred to Svenssen that his were substantially larger than hers. Admittedly he had rather ample man-boobs. Her face, though, could be quite beautiful. Caught in the right light, she looked like Anita Ekberg on a hunger strike.

He noticed to his dismay that the girl was using the cigarette to burn little holes in his duvet cover. "Please don't do that," he said timidly.

She made a fist, as if to box his ears, but then reached over to his nightstand, searching for an ashtray. She found only books.

"You still read this?" She flipped through an old copy of *Pippi Longstocking*.

"One never outgrows Pippi," he said.

"Pippi," the girl said dismissively, "allowed her father to anally rape her."

"I don't recall. Was that in *Pippi Goes to School*?"

The girl didn't answer. She grabbed another paperback from Svenssen's night table. "How about this? Any good?"

It was the latest thriller by Henning Mankell.

"No, I'm afraid it's trash. You can use it as an ashtray."

Svenssen watched the girl smoke down her cigarette. Yes, she might be a clinically insane sociopath, he thought, but he was hardly in a position to complain. At six foot three and 185 pounds, Svenssen was a good deal shorter and fatter than his average male compatriot. Moreover, his complexion looked like Wasa crispbread. It had been a long time since he'd had sex without an exchange of thousands of kronor.

"You know, if you enjoyed it, we could do it again," he said.

"Not now," the girl said. "My vagina feels like raw Baltic salmon."

The expression made him wince. She had few social graces. But there was something refreshing about her candor. "I meant, in the future."

"Maybe." From her black handbag next to the bed she removed her Ericsson Xperia X10 2.1 smartphone with 720p HD video recording and checked her calendar. "Tuesdays are a possibility."

Svenssen checked his Ericsson Xperia X2a with 8.1 megapixel autofocus camera. "I'm afraid Tuesdays I play darts. What about Wednesdays?"

The girl shook her head. "Wednesdays I have kickboxing."

"Thursdays?"

"Krav Maga."

"Fridays?"

"That's when I memorize pi."

After some schedule juggling, they agreed to meet every other Sunday for an hour of semi-consensual intercourse.

"But you must promise to keep this discreet," she said. "I like to keep a low profile."

Just then they noticed Svenssen's neighbor, a seventy-year-old retired stewardess for SAS, observing them from next door through a pair of night-vision binoculars.

Svenssen climbed from the bed and closed the curtains, but not before checking the window thermometer. Minus 37 degrees C. Up a degree from an hour before. Spring was on its way.

He slipped on a linen bathrobe and a pair of clogs and clumped to the kitchen. "Can I offer you some herring?" he called, peering into the fridge. "I have pickled, creamed, fried, kippered, sugar-coated, dollymopped, and licorice-rolled."

The girl had followed him. She was entirely naked but carried an assault rifle. Where did that come from? he wondered. Had it been in her black daypack?

"Must you?" he said. "It makes me quite nervous."

She set the rifle down. "Don't you have any real food?"

Without waiting for an answer, she began rummaging through his cabinets. She had no breasts, no hips, no body fat. Yet she was quite elaborately tattooed. Across the length of her back ran a fastidious reproduction of Rudolph Zallinger's famous *The Age of Dinosaurs* mural in Yale's Peabody Museum. Svenssen recognized it from his graduate student days.

"You like dinosaurs?" he asked.

"These more."

She had found a box of Twinkies. Svenssen blushed. He had a morbid love of American junk food. The more carcinogens and lethal GMOs, the better. Now he watched in astonishment as the emaciated girl stuffed Twinkie after Twinkie in her mouth, swallowing them whole.

"Hungry?" he asked.

"Mmmwm," she said, spewing morsels of cake. When she finished, she grabbed her rifle and headed to Svenssen's study. "C'mon," she said. "Time to get to work."

Blomberg smothered himself between Erotikka Berg's ample and matronly Northern European breasts.

"A kiss for Boo," he said, "and a kiss for Baa."

Boo was slightly larger than Baa.

Erotikka squealed with lusty laughter. "I don't know how you do it, Blomberg. I'm a forty-five-year-old married woman, and you make me feel like a husky in heat."

Blomberg smiled to himself. His twenty-some-year affair with Erotikka was one of the few pleasures in his life these days. Overweight, underexercised, and hirsute in all the wrong places, he was still an amazing chick magnet, but his career as Sweden's leading muckraking journalist was in decline. Last June, Blomberg's magazine, *Millennium*, was purchased by an American media giant. The new publisher, a Harvard MBA with a 500-kronor-a-day cocaine habit, promised to respect the magazine's independence, even after he renamed it *BLINK!* and fired the entire editorial staff. In its place, he hired a team that had previously driven the black salted licorice division of Svenska Fisk AB, producer of the popular Swedish gummy fish, into bankruptcy. Blomberg was asked to drop his multiyear investigation of a vast ring of corruption, prostitution, and ethnic cleansing involving the prime minister and the CEOs of Volvo, Saab, and H&M, and instead to do a story on ABBA's plans to stage a Christmas reunion concert. *Will they or not? Why won't Anni-Frid say?* Blomberg had resigned before he could be fired. Now he wrote his own online blog, Blomsday.

Life in the blogosphere was lonely. His recent piece on former tennis star Matt Wilander's struggle with Nordic Dullness Syndrome (NDS) had been picked up by TV 4 Fakta and Radio Uppsala, but in general Blomberg missed the excitement of writing for a big newsmagazine with a circulation of over 5,000.

He continued to lavish attention on Boo and Baa. After he and Erotikka had achieved multiple simultaneous orgasms, he stretched in bed and said, "How about a nice cup of coffee?"

Erotikka's husband Ralf Berg dutifully rose from his corner of the bed and brought Blomberg a steaming mug with three lumps of sugar, just the way he liked it. Then he retrieved a pack of cigarettes and lit one each for Blomberg and his wife.

"Thanks, Ralf."

"You're welcome, Mikael."

"Thanks, Ralf."

"You're welcome, Erotikka."

Erotikka's husband suspected that Blomberg and Erotikka were having an affair, but he appeared not to mind. He was a firm believer in the Swedish Constitution's Third Amendment, the Right to Free and Multiple Sexual Partners.

"Now, Ralfie," said Erotikka, "be a darling and turn on the tele."

The husband fetched the remote and climbed back into his corner of the bed.

———

The call had come the previous Thursday, out of the blue. Thor's day always brought Professor Dr. Svenssen trouble. He had been in his lab, rearranging birchwood test tubes.

"I'd like to talk to Professor Dr. Sven Svenssen."

"Speaking."

"We need to talk." The voice: girlish, sullen.

"That appears to be what we are doing."

"No, comedian," the voice said urgently. "Not over the phone."

They arranged to meet at his apartment. The girl, wearing a Burton hoodie, arrived on a Powell Skull Deck skateboard. Without so much as a word of greeting, she rode the board into his geo-thermally heated living room and peeled off her clothes. That was before she began to assault him.

Now they sat together in Svenssen's study at his UKEA Real Teak workstation. The girl sat with her knees pinned to her flat chest. She was still naked. The professor admired the rendering of a stegosaurus on her back.

"Maybe we could start," he said, "with you telling me your name."

"Jane Manhater."

Ah, he thought. *A Swedish woman with an American name.* Perhaps that explained her temper. Americans were a violent people. Fourteen thousand gun deaths per annum. A lawless, cultureless, energy-guzzling land of religious fanatics, cowboy politicians, and plutocrats who paid less than 90 percent of their income in taxes.

Still, they did give the world the Twinkie.

"And who do you work for?"

"I told you," the girl named Jane said. "A greeting card firm. Enough questions. Did you look at the file?"

"Yes."

The file had arrived by courier at his lab. The envelope bore no return address, but inside he found a stickie, perhaps someone's oversight: *Manhater Security: Vigilante Specialist and Counter-Patriarchy Mercenary.* At the time he had not been prepared for the file's contents, the graphic photos of mutilation, the blood and tissue samples.

Shoulders lightly touching, they reexamined the grisly evidence.

"Have you identified a cause of death?" she asked.

He nodded. "Strangulation."

"Not decapitation?"

"No. That came later. The victim was already dead."

"Are you certain?"

"Absolutely. She was dead for at least ten hours before they mutilated her."

"They?"

"Just a figure of speech. It could have been one person. I don't know."

The girl glanced at him with her death-black eyes. "Who would do such a thing to a reindeer?"

It was, of course, the same question Svenssen had asked himself. Since becoming chief of Reindeer Forensics at the Royal Pathological Institute in Stockholm in 2003, Svenssen had seen his fair share of reindeer slayings— more than he liked to remember. But nothing quite like this.

"It's hard to say. Two things are for certain, though. First, whoever is responsible is a pro. Secondly, he or *she*"—he added pointedly—"had to be unusually strong."

"How do you know?"

"The victim was strangled by hand."

Svenssen handed a magnifying glass to the naked bipolar security agent with the American name and the dinosaur mural on her back. "Observe these markings on the neck? They were made by fingers. Obviously the killer wore gloves. Possibly hand-knitted mittens. Believe me, it takes a lot of strength to strangle a full-grown reindeer."

The girl nodded. She took notes on her palm. Her nails were painted death-black.

"And the rest?"

"Probably done with a buzz saw. Typically a killer will mutilate a body to hide the evidence. But I don't think so in this case. Otherwise the murderer wouldn't have left the body in the middle of the Stockholm's busiest intersection."

"Right."

"I would guess this killer took pleasure in being brazen. Or maybe he or *she* was trying to send a signal."

"Like what?"

"I don't know. You're the greeting card expert." Svenssen felt satisfaction with his sarcasm.

"Anything else?"

"Yes. She was pregnant."

Erotikka lay on Blomberg's chest. Together they smoked companionably while Blomberg caressed Boo and Baa.

"Ralf, change the channel to the news, would you?"

"Yes, dear."

The breaking news included a report on a bike stolen in Gamla Stan. Fortunately it turned out to be a false alarm. A friend of the bike's owner had borrowed the three-speed without telling his friend. In Norrmalm, a pedestrian was splashed with water while crossing the street. An old man slipped and fell. And in Kungshol-men, an unpublished novelist named Twig Arssen had died of a heart attack at age 50.

Just then Blomberg sat up. "Hey, I knew that guy. We went to journalism school together. He was going to write the Great Swedish Thriller." Dead at fifty. Ouch. Blomberg made a mental note. *Cut back on the fried eel.*

TWO

*In ancient Lappish Land, there existed a rare and powerful
band of women warriors. At puberty, every member of this
fearless tribe attached a third breast, fashioned out of narwhal
blubber, to her abdomen. In this way, she created a handy
shelf where she could store her harpoon.*

—THE YNGLINGA SAGA

Back in her apartment, Lizzy sweated out her rage in her home
sauna and gave herself a deep tissue massage. Then she pulled on
a pair of Scandihoovian cargo pants and sat at her computer, a
Tera 10 mainframe with 544 NovaScale 61-60 servers. The computer, which looked like thirty Viking refrigerators in a row, could
store 1 petabyte of data, more bits of information than there are
gnats in Norrland, and 27 terabytes of memory. Salamander had
bought the computer, recently deaccessioned by the US National
Security Agency, on eBay—outsniping several determined bid-
ders in rural Pakistan.

She liked computers better than humans. They didn't paw her
or play with her tiny nipples like they were ten-kronor coins. And

it felt good to be back at work. The last couple of years had not been easy. Salamander had grown accustomed to a life of abuse, enslavement, and sexual degradation at the hands of her legal guardians. That all changed two years ago when a court declared her more or less sane. But instead of thriving, Salamander had struggled with her new freedom. Money wasn't the problem. She was independently wealthy thanks to hundreds of millions of USD that she'd stolen undetected from the accounts of the world's most detestable billionaire misogynists. But keeping herself occupied was another matter. She opened a vibrator shop in Södermalm, but after a week got bored and destroyed the store with plastic explosives. Then she started a tattoo salon, but her clients complained about the limited options: *I Am a Rapist/Pervert/Pig/ Pederast/Sociopath/Fuckwad/Monster.*

More recently, she had launched her own firm, Manhater Security. She was her own boss and her sole employee. She had even come up with her firm's online advertising campaign: *Suffering from Embarrassing Sexual Predator Problems? Come to Manhater Security. We Punish Early and Often.* She had no clients, but that was fine. She investigated whatever interested her. And the reindeer killings *deeply* interested her.

Her fingers danced over the keyboard with astonishing speed. But her lips, painted with death-black lipstick, were twisted. She hacked her way into all the most obscure search engines—SurfWax, A9, Clicky, BetterBrain, Factbites, Gigablast, iWon, KartOO, Oggleus, Qango, Reftopia. But nothing came up. No real surprise. The search engines were the info-fascists of global capitalism, created to make humanity the sex toys of über-patriarchy.

Next she applied underground analytics, her fingers a blur.

Within minutes, she had found what she was looking for. A dis-ambiguated article about reindeer strangulation on Wikipedia.

Lizzy read to herself, lips quietly forming the words. Reading had not been her strong suit since the second grade, when her teacher touched her forearm and she clubbed him into intensive care.

The Wiki article confirmed her suspicions. This was not the first case involving a strangled female reindeer in Sweden. Twenty years before, at the time of the fall of the Berlin Wall, a reindeer was found hanging from a tree on Gräsö island in Uppland. The body had been discovered by a doctoral student named Goof Graber, who had been researching reindeer family ties at the Royal Center for Advanced Reindeer and Elk Studies in Eskils-tuna.

The Swedish police, working closely with the behaviorists at the Royal Academy of Domestic Nonconformity, issued a psy-chological profile of the kind of Swede who might commit such a ghastly act. Several suspects were taken into custody. A member of the Royal Svensk Polis had notoriously hit one detainee with a collapsible plastic baton, an act of police brutality that led to the collapse of the ruling government and a decade-long disarming of the entire Swedish military.

No solid evidence was ever found against any of the suspects. Years later, the police realized their mistake. All along they as-sumed the killer had been a Swede. They had never seriously weighed the possibility that the reindeer strangler was a foreigner belonging to an ethnic minority. Although Goof Graber had come to Uppsala to study at the famous university, he was born and raised in Oslo, and his parents worked for the Norwegian Cruise

Line. The evidence implicating the Norwegians surfaced too late. Graber had already escaped to the Mexican Riviera on the *Norway Dawn.*

His motive was never entirely clear. Authorities speculated that the killing was part of a coordinated attack on Swedish tourism, designed to raise the fortunes of the then-struggling Norwegian Cruise Line. Others considered him simply a psychopath.

From another Wikipedia article, Lizzy learned that during his time in Eskilstuna, Graber had befriended Dr. Jerker Ekkrot, a leading authority on endangered Baltic sturgeon. It was a name she knew well. Ekkrot had once been arrested for violating the Sex Equality and Dignity Act of 1999. He had called his girlfriend "impractical."

Lizzy grabbed her skateboard and assault rifle. It was time to pay Dr. Ekkrot a visit.

Blomberg heard the familiar coyote howl of *The Good, the Bad, and the Ugly.* It was the ringtone of his HTC Evo 4G cell phone with an 8-megapixel camera with HD-video-recording capabilities and a 1GHz Snapdragon processor.

"Hello, I'd like to speak to speak to Mikael Blomberg."

"Speaking."

"Mr. Blomberg, my name is Nix Arssen, the father of Twig Arssen. As you might have heard, my son was found dead yesterday."

"Yes, I'm very sorry."

"I'm not calling for condolences. To be honest, my relationship with my son deteriorated after his third birthday. But I understand you and Twig studied together. I'd like to talk. In person."

An hour later they met at Mellqvists Kaffebar. It was a popular hangout with the Fågelås biker scene. Twig's father was medium height. His face was that of a nondescript retiree of seventy. He had hair, eyes, etc. A waiter took their order.

"I'd like a coffee," said Blomberg.

"Tall, extra-tall, or trough?"

"Trough, please."

"Make that two troughs," said Arssen. Then he turned to Blomberg. "It's good of you to come."

"So what is it that you wanted to discuss?"

"I know things haven't been easy for you professionally," said Nix Arssen. "I used to read all your exposés about tax fraud, pedophilia, and heroin smuggling in the highest echelons of Swedish business. But as I recall, you used to publish under a different surname."

"True. Back then I was Mikael Blomquvist. Recently I discovered my Jewish roots. I learned that my ancestors came to Sweden during the liberal reign of dowager queen Hedvig Eleonora of Holstein-Gottorp. So I changed my name back to the original. But we're not here to talk about me, are we?"

"I suppose not. Permit me, though, to say that it is a sad commentary on our world when the great Mikael Blomberg is reduced to writing about ABBA's reunion concert for *BLINK!*"

"Which is why I quit."

"Now I follow your blog. I never knew about Matt Wilander's struggle with chronic dullness."

"It's an overlooked disease. It affects millions of Swedes."

"I can't imagine, though, that writing a daily blog pays the bills on your Volvo S60 with all-wheel drive."

Blomberg wondered how he knew about the all-wheel drive.

Arssen must have seen Blomberg park his Volvo in front of the café. The fact was that Blomberg had looked into trading the S60 in for a S40 without turbo and AWD. He would miss the firm seats of the S60, but he could save 120 kronor a month in petrol costs.

"Mikael, let me be frank. I'd like to hire you."

"To do what?"

"As you know, my son never experienced much success as a writer of thrillers. He dreamed of having a great bestseller in America, so he set all his stories in far-flung locales—Paris, Rome, New York. Little did he know that Americans in their inestimable stupidity prefer thrillers set in northern Lapland. Sadly, he never even found an agent."

Blomberg nodded. He recalled that Twig had always been an atrocious writer. Functionally Illiterate Twig had been his nickname in journalism school. Unpublishable Twig.

"At the end of his life, my son was working on a manuscript that he thought would be his big breakout. Last night, when I examined his apartment, I couldn't find any trace of it."

"So you want me to find the missing manuscript."

"I could handsomely remunerate you."

"What does that mean?"

"Remunerate is a verb. It means 'to pay' or 'to compensate for services rendered.'"

"I meant how much."

"Twenty-five hundred kronor per day."

Blomberg did the mental math. That was ten times as much as he earned on his daily blog.

"And, of course, I'd like you to find my son's killer."

"Killer? I thought he died of a heart attack."

Arssen shook his head. "Please, come with me."

Chief Inspector Svenjamin Bubbles of the Royal Svensk Polis ducked under the police tape that surrounded the modest 1,700-square-foot house heated by natural gas. He found Officer Stamer Flunk taking notes by the front door.

"Where's Ekkrot?"

"Which part?"

"That bad?"

"Worse."

"Let's start with the torso."

"Bedroom"

"Head?"

"Dining room table."

"Genitals?"

"Still looking."

Bubbles squinted into the gale force wind and turned up the collar of his coat. It was −45 degrees. *Should have brought my hat.* "Well, let's take a look."

Inside, the house looked surprisingly large, more like 1,900 square feet or even 2,000. Maybe this had something to do with the walls, which were sprayed brightly by blood, as was the UKEA bookcase. Prominently displayed was Ekkrot's most famous book. In its day, *The Life Cycle of the Baltic Sturgeon, with Particular Attention to Matters of Coastline Breeding* had been a bestseller, and it remained a contemporary Swedish classic. Bubbles had caught some of the early reviews and for years had kept the book on his UKEA nightstand without ever reading it.

Now I really should get around to it, thought the chief inspector as he examined the author's torso. It had been shockingly mutilated. Little remained to identify this as a human being, though the decapitation had been remarkably clean.

"Suicide?" asked Officer Flunk.

Bubbles took a swig of the Pepto-Bismol that he kept in a silver pocket flask. Since joining the force fifteen years ago, he'd noticed a steady decline in the quality of police recruits. The force was no longer the elite unit that had once been the envy of the subarctic circle. Much as he hated to admit it, he feared that immigration played a role. As one of the eight Jews in this Lutheran nation, Bubbles was proud of the police force's multiculturalism. Still, he couldn't help but note that Flunk was an ethnic Finn. Vividly he remembered the words of his instructor in ethnic diversity at the Royal Police Academy. "Finns are a touchy people. They have been shown to lack basic deductive and analogical reasoning abilities. Their average performance on the Scandinavian Aptitude Test is almost as low as that of the Danes, a frivolous people who struggle with logical thinking, particularly during the winter months. The Icelanders, by contrast, display problems common to a people subjected to generations of inbreeding. They are genetically prone to lying and thievery."

"Did you find a note?" Bubbles's voice was laced with sarcasm.

"No," the officer admitted sheepishly.

As Bubbles continued to examine the crime scene, something made his heart skip a beat and the hair on the back of his neck stand up. Next to the torso was a silver eyebrow stud in the shape of a lizard.

"Not just any lizard," he whispered to himself. "A *salamander*."

THREE

The Swedish language had no word for laughter until 1855.
— FOLKETS LEXIKON SVENSKA

Arssen drove Blomberg to the Olaf Palme Forensic Institute for Crime Solution in his Volvo V70 turbo. They stopped once along the way to fix leaking antifreeze. At the institute they were met by the chief medical examiner. Blomberg immediately recognized him. Two years ago, Dr. Ink Nyquill had assisted in operating on Lizzy Salamander after she'd been shot multiple times point-blank in the head. Fortunately, the bullets had left Salamander with no brain damage, and in fact appeared to have strengthened her computational powers and her endgame in chess.

Blomberg and Nyquill shook hands. "It's good to see you again," the doctor said. "I enjoyed your piece on Wilander and Nordic Dullness Syndrome. It's about time that both the public and the medical community took NDS more seriously. I understand you knew the deceased?"

They stood by a body covered with a sheet.

Blomberg nodded. "We were students together." Confidentially he added, "Never much of a writer, but something of an athlete. He won the five-kilometer permafrost run."

"I'm afraid he let himself go since his student days. The autopsy and blood work tell a sad story. Cholesterol well above 350, triglycerides over 500, massive calcification of the superior vena cava, midstage sclerosis of the liver. Elevated levels of bilirubin, ammonia, hydroxyprogesterone, and urea nitrogen. His CD4 cell count was abnormal, as were his amylase values and his ceruloplasmin."

Blomberg examined the charts. "I guess these values also indicate a morbidly depressed osmolality and dangerously high concentrations of globulin. And I take it his mean corpuscular hemoglobin concentration also raises a red flag."

The doctor glanced at Blomberg, visibly impressed.

"I once did an exposé about money-laundering, sex slavery, and human embryo harvesting in Sweden's largest blood-testing firm," Blomberg volunteered.

"Based on these tests," Dr. Nyquill said, "I would say that the deceased smoked on average sixty cigarettes a day, drank twenty cups of coffee, ingested five liters of beer, and subsisted entirely on Rancho Diablo Taco Beef Fritter Chips and fried eel. I'd be surprised if he'd done anything more aerobic than nap in his Stressless chair for the last twenty years."

This brought Blomberg up short. He swallowed hard. It sounded a great deal like his own daily regimen. He would have to cut back to fifteen cups of coffee a day. *And no fried eel.* "So he died of a heart attack?"

"That's what I thought. Until I noticed this."

Nyquill pulled back the sheet on the cadaver. Blomberg gasped. His friend was unrecognizable from their student days. His body, once taut and muscular, looked pale and bloated. He had gained at least forty pounds. And back then he'd had a head. Now all that remained was a clean space above his neck.

"Decapitated," Blomberg said.

"Yes," the doctor confirmed. "And there's something else you should know. Whoever decapitated your friend didn't use a chain saw. I've never quite seen a decapitation like this. The trachea was perfectly severed. The killer clearly knew his anatomy."

"So we're looking for a psychopathic serial killer who's probably also a world-class surgeon."

"I believe so. That, or an experienced samurai warrior."

Salamander sat at Afhild's, a kaffeklub popular with the Torbjörntorp jazz scene, gargling espresso.

She was in a foul mood. She had lost her favorite salamander eyebrow ring. She had bought the ring as a gift to herself after she successfully siphoned an additional 150 million kronor from the offshore account of Sweden's most violently misogynistic hedge-fund manager. Last week she'd lost a tongue stud. She was becoming forgetful, absentminded. Maybe it was the legacy of years spent strapped immobile to a gurney being force-fed mind-altering drugs—not to mention getting shot repeatedly in the brain by family members.

At the next table sat a bickering American couple. "I don't want to see another old boat," the wife complained.

"It's *not* an *old boat*," the husband said. "It's one of the great maritime museums in the world."

"That's the *same* thing you said about that bore in Copenhagen."

"This one's better. I promise."

"But what about the adorable little boutiques we passed this morning? I'm dying to buy one of those original hand-painted wooden horses."

"We have all day tomorrow for shopping."

As they continued to argue, Salamander noticed the man had slung his daypack over the back of his chair. Casually Salamander leaned over and pickpocketed his iPhone 4 with GSM/EDGE, 1900 MHz. It took her thirty seconds to hack into his Facebook, Twitter, email, and Merrill Lynch accounts, and another thirty seconds to memorize thousands of pages of personal communications and complex financial transactions. At least her memory was still intact. The man's name was Harvey Hirsch, an American orthodontist. In the past year, Hirsch had earned 97,000 USD, but had paid only 24,000 USD in taxes. *No wonder that sick country has no high-speed rail system.* His wife's name was Alison. She sold low-carb cookies in a shop that measured 550 square feet, not including the double-door entranceway. Many of Hirsch's emails were to a woman named Jennifer. One said, <I could do a short lunch on the 20th at 1 p.m.>

So the fuckwad's having an affair right under his wife's nose with his minister's underage daughter.

Just then Salamander noticed that the man had stood up; his hands were moving to the woman's neck. *Whoa. Dickface is going to murder his wife right in the middle of Afhild's. The chutzpah.*

In a flash, Salamander was on her feet. "Bad move, wife-battering pigdog," she whispered under her breath. "Prepare to die."

She grabbed a chair and smashed it over an empty table until she was left with a single leg. Holding it like a baseball bat— Salamander admired American sports, motorcycles, and Twinkies, but not wife-raping evangelical freaks—she gave a mighty swing, connecting squarely with the man's right temple. He crumpled, same as all the men Salamander had struck in the head with blunt force.

In a moment she was on him. Blow after blow landed on the man's face, neck, and crotch.

"Jesus!" the wife screamed. "Leave my husband alone, you scrawny punk!"

Salamander understood the psychology all too intimately: women who, having suffered decades of brutality at the hands of sociopathic beasts, come to identify with their tormentors. It wasn't called the Stockholm syndrome for nothing.

"Help!" screamed the pathetic wife. "She's going to kill him."

Salamander landed one final blow cleanly between the man's eyes and tossed the battered chair leg to the ground. *No more child porn for you, dildo breath.* She was sweating, but sighed with satisfaction. She heard the wife crying to the maître d', "My husband was helping me with the clasp of my new rune necklace, and this girl at the next table went totally berserk."

Salamander calmly took her black leather jacket and left the restaurant. She deposited the man's iPhone in a trash bin, but not before wiping it down for fingerprints. She sighed to herself. *Poor Alison. One day she'll thank me for saving her life.*

Blomberg and Arssen were back in Mellqvists Kaffebar, lapping from troughs of Ukrainian cappuccino.

"It looks like a psychopathic surgeon may have decapitated your son," Blomberg said. "That or a highly skilled samurai swordsman."

Arssen shook his head. "I don't believe so."

"Why? Did Twig have any enemies?"

"I don't exactly know. As I've said, our relations had been strained since his third birthday, when I bought him a toy Volvo P210 that turned out to have defective steering. But it's possible that while researching his book, Twig had uncovered some dangerous information. I was hoping he might have confided in you, as you were his dearest friend."

"I hadn't seen him in twenty-five years," Blomberg said. "Even back then, we never spoke."

"Twig liked to keep to himself. He was a guarded person. This is somewhat understandable given the history of our family. You see, Twig's grandfather—my father, Odder—was born in the north, above the Arctic Circle. He was one of seventeen boys, but tragically the only one to survive past his second birthday. All his siblings died of crib death. Back then, mothers didn't know the health risks of letting their infants sleep with pillows pressed over their faces. My grandmother understandably took the death of her sixteen infant boys hard, and spent the last decades of her life in a prison for the criminally insane.

"Father's father was a skilled carpenter and a strict Lutheran who believed in the strap, if you understand my meaning," Arssen went on. "He raised Father to be a carpenter too, but Father rebelled against the religious strictness and the constant beatings. World War I had just ended, and Father ran away. He was young, an excellent runner, and he ran all the way to Germany. This naturally took several weeks, as he first had to cross Finland, Russia, Estonia, Latvia, Lithuania, and Poland. He finally stopped in Munich. By then his leather sneakers were entirely worn through. There he met a virulently anti-Semitic unemployed bohemian who had dreams of becoming an artist but who'd twice been rejected by Vienna's prestigious Academy of Visual Arts."

"Hitler."

"Exactly. At the time, Hitler was supporting himself by selling kitschy watercolors, essentially living on the streets, spending his days in beer halls, talking radical politics. My father fell completely under Hitler's sway. In fact, Father was the first one to call him *mein Führer*. Later, of course, Hitler's plans would change, but this was still early in his career, and his newest dream was to open a furniture store, Führer's Furniture.

"Hitler would do the designs," Arssen continued after a prolonged slurp, "and Father would handle the building. They started with simple office and household pieces—coffee tables, bookcases, desk chairs. Nice functional items. Unfortunately this was during the terrible inflation, and very few Germans could afford a nightstand that cost eight trillion marks. If the store had succeeded, the world might have been spared considerable misery. But business was bad, and Hitler's ambitions turned from furniture to global conquest. After the store folded, Father, ever loyal to the Führer, followed Hitler into politics and became a fervent Nazi. In 1942, Hitler appointed him the head of the Ministry of Aryan Carpentry in the Third Reich. Father occupied this position until Germany's unconditional surrender. After the war ended, he escaped back to Sweden, where he joined up with thousands of other Swedes who had worked with the Third Reich either at home or abroad. He was penniless, but he still had saved all the furniture designs that Hitler had drawn during the days of their business. Claiming these as his own, he sold them to Sløber Ukea, who had a dream of starting a business that would supply inexpensive furniture to a continent recovering from catastrophic war. These designs proved highly popular, and Sløber Ukea hired Father as one of his firm's first master carpenters."

Blomberg looked up from his trough. "Let me see if I have this right. Are you telling me that for the last sixty years UKEA has been building furniture designed by Adolf Hitler?"

"Exactly."

"Did Twig know this?"

"I tried to keep the family history secret. I kept everything in a locked file cabinet at home labeled 'Unspeakable Family Secrets: Do Not Open.' But it's possible he learned something. Twig liked to snoop around."

"Do you have Hitler's furniture sketches?"

"No. Those would all be in the corporate archives of UKEA."

"Do you have any idea what his missing manuscript was about?"

"At first I assumed it was another thriller. I never spoke to my son about his writing. I thought he might more profitably try his hand at a postmodern family romance, like the American Jonathan Franzen. But Twig was stubborn. Now I've come to believe that the book was a nonfictional account of this dangerous history. He sent me one postcard about his project. I have it here."

Blomberg examined the postcard. On the front was a picture of a modern utilitarian building, UKEA Corporate Archives. The writing on the back was small and neat.

Dear Father, I'm making good progress on my new book. I am hopeful it will attract attention in America, as this time I've found a Swedish angle. Maybe it will even have a hardback edition. I fear, though, that it will cost me my life, bring down the ruling government, and lead to the collapse of the Swedish state.

Best, Twig

Chief Inspector Bubbles stepped over the police tape that sealed off Twig Arssen's apartment. Why would anyone want to decapitate an unpublished author of Swedish thrillers? And there was Ekkrot to think about. Two decapitations in a single week. A trained surgeon—or samurai—serial killer on the loose. *Just as I was thinking about taking off a week for a little R&R in Greenland.*

Bubbles nodded at Officer Nemo Snorkkle. "So what have you got?" he asked coolly. Snorkkle was not Bubbles's favorite cop on the force. Although not nearly as stupid as Officer Flunk, the ethnic Finn, Snorkkle was part Lap, and so prone to irrationality and spontaneous outbursts of violence. Bubbles didn't like the way he fondled his service revolver, even if it only fired caps. Last year a patrolman's standard issue 9-millimeter Sig Sauer accidentally discharged, puncturing the front tire of a parked Saab. The uproar led to a national referendum in which an overwhelming majority of Swedes voted to restrict police firearms to squirt, cap, and paintball guns. The police also now had to wear cable-knit sweaters of organically dyed wool.

"We were going over Arssen's apartment. We found this."

Snorkkle showed Bubbles a tiny glass aperture in the wall across from the door into the writer's apartment.

"A surveillance camera?"

"Yes. The camera itself is hidden in Arssen's clothes closet. There's another in his bedroom and one more in the bathroom."

"For homemade porn?" asked the inspector.

"I don't think so. I found a receipt on his dresser. The cameras were installed by Milksop Security only two weeks before Arssen's murder."

Bubbles knew Milksop well. It was run by Radovan Armanskovitzdullah, the son of an Estonian-Serbian-Mongolian-Senegalese jazz saxophonist and a Cambodian-Sumatran-Tanzanian-Ukrainian double agent. Part Muslim, part Jew, and part Papua New Guinea wigman, Armanskovitzdullah also constituted the entire board of directors of Stockholm's new multicultural center. Blomberg and Armanskovitzdullah often played chess together while drinking skinny lattes and eating herring-flavored licorice.

"Why would an unpublished writer wire his apartment with state-of-the-art security cameras?" Bubbles said.

Bubbles and Snorkkle were joined by Officer Flunk. "Maybe he feared falling random victim to a serial decapitator," the latter speculated.

"Foolish Finn," Snorkkle muttered under his breath.

"I won't tolerate ethnic slurs," said Bubbles. Inwardly, though, he entertained hurtful stereotypes. *Obviously there are intelligent Finns, but on aggregate they really are exceptionally stupid. And they've produced nothing of lasting cultural value except some colorful bedsheets.*

"Have you checked to see if the cameras were working on the evening of the murder?" Bubbles asked.

"It looks like they were," said Snorkkle.

"Then we just might have our killer on tape," said Bubbles. "Get the cameras. We'll watch back at the station."

"Mr. Blomberg, it's a great pleasure to meet you," said Dagher Ukea, the CEO of UKEA AB. Blomberg sat in the CEO's plush 320-square-foot office at UKEA's world corporate headquarters. Ukea was tall, and for a man of sixty, exceptionally well preserved. His eyes were polar ice blue, and his hair polar bear white. His nails gleamed from his morning manicure. Ukea lightly touched his fingertips together in a sign of conspiratorial corporate evil. "I've admired your work for many years. I always eagerly read your exposés of insider trading, fornication, and treason at the highest levels of corporate Sweden. I recall, though, that back then your byline was—how shall I put it?—less *ethnic* in character." Ukea smiled thinly.

"I recently changed my name after discovering my family's Jewish roots. My ancestors came to Sweden during the liberal reign of dowager queen Hedvig Eleonora of Holstein-Gottorp."

"Hedvig was a most tolerant dowager," Ukea said, again lightly touching his fingers and smiling maliciously. "I recall glancing at your recent blog on Matt Wilander's struggles with Nordic Dullness Syndrome."

"It's a real disease. It strikes many Swedes."

"I don't doubt it. I myself always preferred Stefan Edberg to Wilander." Ukea stared coldly. "But Ivan Lendl was my favorite player."

"Yes, Lendl," Blomberg said. He remembered Lendl and his sweeping one-handed backhand well. *The surliest cyborg ever to be ranked number one in the world.*

"But we're not here to talk about tennis, are we? You say you're on an assignment. I'm glad to know that the great Mikael Blomquvist—"

"—berg."

"Yes, excuse me"—Ukea flashed another toxic, small-toothed smile—"in any case, it's good to know that you're back writing for serious print journalism."

"Actually, it's a private assignment."

"*Private . . .* I see." His lips curled in schadenfreude. Blomberg noticed that a Persian cat had suddenly appeared on Ukea's lap. The CEO stroked it languidly. The cat eyed Blomberg with visible malice. "Well, work is work, isn't it?"

"That's how I see it," Blomberg said. He glanced at the framed pictures displayed on the CEO's desk. Ukea shaking hands with George Steinbrenner; Ukea toasting Gordon Gekko; Ukea embracing Charles Montgomery Burns.

"Remind me. The assignment comes from?"

"Twig Arssen's father."

The cat hissed ferociously.

"There, there, kitty," said Ukea. "Ah, I read about the son's death. A most unfortunate decapitation."

"I understand that Twig's grandfather worked for UKEA."

"Yes, Odder Arssen was a most skilled designer. Until he went insane."

"Arssen went insane?"

"But of course!" Ukea cried. The cat purred madly. "Here, take a look." From the top drawer of his UKEA desk Ukea removed a folder and handed it to Blomberg.

It was titled, "Arssen, Odder: Insanity of."

Curious that he had the folder at the ready.

Blomberg flipped through the file. It was at least fifty pages long. He quickly scanned the diagnosis. *Paranoid schizophrenia. Multiple personality disorder. Bipolar kleptomania. Egodystonic homosexuality disorder. Attention-deficit/hyperactivity disorder. Munchausen syndrome. Self-defeating personality disorder. Premenstrual dysphoric disorder.* He noticed the report was signed by Dr. Madder Tele-pathian, the same psychiatrist who had once diagnosed Lizzy Salamander.

"Was Arssen ever institutionalized?"

"We had no choice. He was dreadfully delusional. He accused our coffee-table division of perpetrating crimes against humanity." Ukea could not suppress a small laugh. "The inanity of it all—the makers of coffee tables implicated in such unspeakable crimes! We couldn't tolerate these accusations any longer. They were eroding morale. The quality of our tables began to suffer."

"Where was the hospital?"

"Why, right here, naturally."

"UKEA maintains its own psychiatric institution?"

"Of course. We believe it is our responsibility to take care of those employees who cannot cope with the inevitable stresses of our workplace. It is part of being a caring corporation." Ukea fondled a diamond-studded Montblanc fountain pen.

"May I visit this facility?"

"Impossible. There's only *one way* to gain admittance, if you catch my meaning."

The cat swatted at the pen with her long claws.

"Would it be possible to examine your firm's archives?"

"By all means." Ukea laughed expansively, as did the cat. "But I'm afraid you'll find very little of interest. We run a squeaky clean operation here at UKEA. All quite dull. Matt Wilander would feel very much at home."

FOUR

MÅNDAG, JANUARI 17–TORSDAG, JANUARI 20

Between the years 1500 and 2000, the rate of violent crime in Sweden (including murder and rape) increased by 46%.
—ROYAL STATISTICAL ABSTRACT FOR SWEDEN, WITH PARTICULAR ATTENTION TO THE NORRBOTTEN TUNDRA, 1310–2010

"Are we ready to watch the video?" Chief Inspector Bubbles asked.

"I think so," said Officer Flunk. He pressed the play button on the video camera. Nothing appeared on the computer monitor. Bubbles noticed that the video camera was simply sitting next to the officer's desktop computer.

"Are we hooked up by Bluetooth?" he asked.

Flunk looked at Officer Snorkkle. They both shrugged.

"Then don't we need a USB cable to hook the camera to the computer?" Bubbles said.

Flunk and Snorkkle searched the police headquarters.

"We don't seem to have such a cable."

"Then maybe we need to buy one." Bubbles tried to control the tremor of rage in his voice.

"What kind of cable did you say, sir?"

"USB."

Flunk wrote this on the back of his hand.

"You can get it at any electronics store," Bubbles added.

"I'll get right on it, sir."

Just then Flunk's cellphone chirped. He spoke quietly for several minutes.

"Excuse me, sir. That was my domestic partner. Today is my day to pick up our girl from day care. Would you mind if I first swung by the day-care center before I buy the"—he glanced down at his hand—"USB cable."

"That's fine, Flunk."

"Don't stores close early today?" Officer Snorkkle said. "Isn't it Maundy Monday? I'm sorry, sir."

Snorkkle always apologized to Bubbles any time there was a Christian holiday. Snorkkle bent over backward to remember every Jewish holiday, never failing to give his boss a spice cake that he bought at a bakery in Gamla Stan. ("Merry Yom Kippur, Chief Inspector!" "Why, thank you, Officer Snorkkle. A spice cake! How thoughtful!")

Bubbles checked his calendar. "You're right. Shops close today at two."

It was already one-thirty.

"If I'm late for the pickup, the day care fines us," Flunk said. "Ten kronor per minute."

Snorkkle whistled. "Pretty steep."

"Don't worry, Flunk," said Bubbles. "The department will cover the charge."

Flunk shifted his feet uneasily. "It's not just the money. The day care will call home. My partner will be furious."

"Do your best, Flunk. But get a move on it."

"Yes, sir."

Blomberg sat in the rectangular 1,015-square-foot main reading room of the UKEA corporate archive. An archivist silently approached him on slippered feet. Her hair was pinned back severely. She had eyes like an Alaskan Malamute, one brown and one light blue. "How may I help you?"

"I'd like to see the original design of the Kackerlacka junior chair."

The archivist held a finger to her lips. She wore white cotton gloves. "Silence! This is a study area."

Blomberg glanced around. The reading room was completely empty except for four other archivists stationed at each corner of the room, watching them intently.

"I'm sorry," Blomberg whispered. "The Kackerlacka junior chair sketches, please."

"All requests must be filled out in writing."

She directed Blomberg's attention to an even stack of request forms collected in a box on the table.

Blomberg filled out the form and handed it to the archivist. She returned a half hour later with the file: "Kackerlacka Junior Chair: Original Sketch and Design."

The file was empty.

He handed it back to the archivist. "May I request another?"

"Certainly."

"I'd like to see—"

"Requests must be in writing!"

He filled out a new form for the Arisk children's table. A half hour later, the archivist returned. The file was also empty.

Next Blomberg requested the Snåljåp side table. Empty. The Herrefolk bookcase. Nothing. The Härskarras buffet. Blank.

After several hours, he'd grown weary.

"Any additional requests?"

"No, I'm good. Thank you."

The archivist nodded graciously.

But just as he was handing back the file of the Ljushårig queen-size bed with matching dresser, he noticed faint writing impressed in the corner of the folder. Nonchalantly he snapped a picture of the impression with his Xperia X10 droid smartphone. An hour later, back in his apartment, Blomberg enlarged the image on his 17-inch Apple G4. The writing, despite the attempt to erase it, was perfectly clear. *Originalahornholzdoppelbettentwurf von AH.* "Original design of maplewood double bed by AH."

Flunk unwrapped the USB cable and searched for the proper port on the computer.

"It's the one with the trident symbol," Bubbles said.

"Trident?" repeated Flunk doubtfully.

"Pitchfork," said Bubbles. He discreetly swigged from his flask of Pepto-Bismol. *The Finns lack a rich vocabulary.*

"Okay, got it."

"Pappa, can I have something to drink?" This came from Flunk's five-year-old daughter, Brigitta.

"What would you like, sweetheart?"

"A glass of mjölk!"

Snorkkle checked in the office refrigerator. He shook his head.

"No mjölk," said Flunk. "How about something else?"

"I want mjölk!" the girl shrieked.

"We usually keep some mjölk for our coffee," Bubbles said.

"I think we used the last of it this morning," said Snorkkle.

"If you knew that, why didn't you get more?" asked Bubbles.

"It slipped my mind," said Snorkkle.

"There's nothing we can do about that now," said Flunk. "All the shops are closed."

"There must be a Konsume still open in Drottninggatan," Bubbles said.

"I'll check," said Snorkkle, grabbing his coat.

"Why don't you call first?" suggested Bubbles.

"Good idea." After a couple of calls, Snorkkle found an open convenience store. "They have both regular mjölk and choklad mjölk. Which would you like?"

"Choklad mjölk!" squealed the girl.

"What do you say?" said her father.

"Please."

While Snorkkle was out shopping, Chief Inspector Bubbles got out the box of emergency toys. Personally Bubbles preferred Playmobil figures, but a number of parents had protested the force's endorsement of plastic toys made in Germany, and so the force had replaced them with nonviolent Brio figures made of wood.

Still, Bubbles hadn't been able to bring himself to discard the set of Playmobil police.

Sitting on the floor with Brigitta, he tried to settle a hostage situation.

"Bang, bang! You're dead!" cried Brigitta. Her Playmobil police officer brandished a weapon.

"It's better to negotiate," Bubbles gently admonished.

Brigitta grabbed the tiny megaphone from Bubbles's Playmobil sergeant and threw it angrily across the room. "No negotiating with terrorists!" the girl screamed. "It's time to act!"

Fortunately just then Snorkkle returned with the choklad mjölk, a twelve-pack of sippy boxes. Straws inserted into their boxes, the officers prepared to watch the video.

"Pappa, I want to watch, too."

"Now, sweetheart, what did I tell you about watching decapitations?"

"I don't care. I want to watch!"

A tantrum ensued. Finally the officers gave in.

"But Pappa's going to cover your eyes if they're any bad parts, okay?"

"No!"

The security camera had been connected to Arssen's front door, and so the video began with him answering a persistent knock. Bubbles took careful notes of what he saw.

Arssen opens door. On the threshold stands a short girl, maybe 17 or 18. She wears a black T-shirt of Tweety Bird holding an automatic weapon (AK-47?). Tweety Bird's speech bubble says, "Prepare to Die, Puddy Fucking Cat." Assailant enters Arssen's apartment. Arssen retreats, fearful. Assailant reaches behind her back and unsheathes a samurai sword (carbonized steel?). Height: not above 4'11". Weight: 90 to 95 pounds. Hair: death-black. Eyes: ditto. Heavily tattooed and ringed. She runs effortlessly around the walls and ceiling of Arssen's central hall. Victim retreats, now visibly terrified. She mouths words: Prepare to die, Twig Fucking Arssen! *(Check with staff lip-reader?) Assailant swings sword.*

"Pappa! I wanna watch!"

Victim's head flies off, bounces several times on the hardwood floor (ash? oak?), and comes to a stop. Assailant takes black marker and draws what looks like a soccer goal on hallway wall. She retreats as if to take a penalty, then runs up and swiftly kicks the head against the wall.

"GOAL!!!!!" cried Brigitta.

Assailant disappears into another room. Reappears moments later. Her daypack (Tumi?) now looks full; she may have stolen something, perhaps a laptop. Before leaving, she walks straight to the surveillance camera and sticks out her middle figure. Mouths an expletive. Exits.

"My God, I recognize that face!" cried Officer Flunk. "Isn't that the girl from *Sweden's Got Talent?*"

"More like Sweden's Got Psychopaths," snarled Snorkkle. "It's that rancid punk who was buried alive by her own father at a family reunion."

Bubbles swallowed hard. From the top drawer of his desk, he removed the silver eyebrow stud he had found at the Ekkrot crime scene.

"Look at the pretty gecko pin," said Brigitta.

"That's no gecko," said Bubbles quietly. Then to Officer Snorkkle he said, "Issue an arrest warrant for Lizzy Salamander. Wanted for the murders of Dr. Jerker Ekkrot and unpublished writer Twig Arssen. Suspect is armed and extremely dangerous . . . especially to men."

Snorkkle twittered the message to the other five members of the Swedish police. Under his breath he said, "This time we're going to nail that psychopathic cunt."

Blomberg and Erotikka were lying in bed.

Erotikka pouted. "You love Boo more than Baa."

"Don't be ridiculous. I love Boo and Baa equally."

"Baa feels neglected."

"Poor Baa. Do you feel neglected?" He smothered Baa with adoring kisses.

Erotikka threw her arms around his neck. "I don't know what it is about you, but you make me feel like an elk in estrus."

Blomberg smiled thinly. Frankly Erotikka's appetites were starting to exhaust him.

"Let's stay in bed all day," she purred. "It's too cold to get up."

Blomberg checked the temperature on his titanium HTC-HD71GHz Snapdragon CPU smartphone. A brisk −58 degrees. Outside it was colder still. They had driven north of Stockholm to Blomberg's 270-square-foot shågshäck on Lake Fikmisst. Because of the open floor plan, Erotikka felt it was more like 340 square feet.

Blomberg sat up in bed, lit a cigarette, and drank coffee from a thermos he kept on his nightstand.

"What's wrong?" Erotikka said.

Blomberg shrugged. "I know it sounds ridiculous, but suddenly I don't like being surrounded by all this UKEA furniture." He glanced at his UKEA headboard, UKEA nightstand, UKEA dresser, UKEA rocking chair, UKEA shoe organizer, UKEA change tray, and UKEA sexual enhancement stool. Even his reindeer night-light was UKEA.

"Does the thought that all this might have been designed by Adolf Hitler bother you?"

"It does."

"But these designs are from last year's fall catalog."

"That's not the point. They all go back to those first sketches. I can't get over the idea that UKEA's inexpensive, no-nonsense self-assembly bookcases used Hitler's designs."

"Later his taste became so grandiose."

"That was in part Albert Speer's influence." Blomberg fell silent, then said quietly. "Imagine—if Twig's unpublished manuscript was going to blow the whistle on UKEA, think how many people would want him dead. His murder probably implicates persons in the highest positions."

"You don't have any hard evidence."

"Just the story that his father told me. And that erased label I found at the UKEA archives."

"What about the manuscript?"

"It appears to have disappeared."

Just then Ralf, Erotikka's husband, spoke up. "You should take a look at this." He'd been curled on a corner of the bed, without blankets, reading the newspaper on his Mobilglide P-3300 2GHz smartphone. He handed it to Blomberg.

The headline was from the *Aftonbladet*:

POLICE NAME LIZZY SALAMANDER PRINCIPAL SUSPECT IN MURDERS OF STURGEON EXPERT AND UNPUBLISHED THRILLER WRITER.

WTF, Blomberg thought. *Oh, Lizzy, not again.*

Blomberg entered Chief Inspector Bubbles's office without knocking. Bubbles rose with his hand extended in greeting.

"What a surprise. We missed you at shul last weekend."

"I had to finish my blog. Did we have a minyan?"

"Fortunately we were able to find some Dutch tourists."

Bubbles and Blomberg both belonged to Adat Jisrael, a small synagogue that served all eight Jews who lived north of 59 degrees latitude. They were also close friends, though this hadn't always been the case. Several years ago, when Blomberg still wrote for *Millennium,* they had almost come to blows about an exposé that Blomberg had written about corruption, prostitution, and drug trafficking in the police's Bureau of Special Investigations into Corruption, Prostitution, and Drug Trafficking.

"So to what do I owe the honor of this visit?" Bubbles said. "Let me guess: it has something to do with your friend, the killer."

"I can't really call her a friend. I haven't seen Salamander in two years. But I do wonder what you guys at the force have against her."

In the last five years, the police had arrested Salamander thirty-two times, but the charges—which included everything to shoplifting black lipstick from the Goth boutique in Holdershalm to plotting the extermination of the male population of Northern Europe—had never stuck. It invariably turned out that her acts of violence had been committed in retaliation, though some members of the force openly wondered how preemptive castration could be considered self-defense. Officer Snorkkle was among the doubters. Just then Snorkkle peered into Inspector Bubbles's office and screamed, "This time we're going to nail that satanic cunt to the fucking wall!"

"We're quite confident," said Bubbles to Blomberg, "that we finally have solid evidence against your four-foot-ten psychopath. Irrefutable evidence. Evidence that would turn even the most die-hard Salamander defender into a believer."

"Really? What kind of evidence?"

Bubbles laughed. "Do you think I'd tip my hand to Sweden's most popular blogger?"

"I'm hardly the most popular. That would be volvo_recall.se. But I am in the top hundred. And you've done it before."

"True. But only if you give me what you've got. Assuming you've got something."

"What do you think?"

"Okay, pull up a chair."

After watching the video for the second time, Blomberg sat speechless.

"So you see," said Bubbles. "Pretty nasty stuff. I assume you don't know where we might be able to find Fröken Salamander."

"As I've said, I haven't seen her in over two years." Blomberg shook his head as if to rid himself of the disturbing images he'd just seen. "I just don't understand it. What could be her motive?"

"Revenge?" Bubbles offered.

"I've never known Lizzy Salamander to be a vengeful person."

For a moment Blomberg and the inspector sat in silence. Then, as if on cue, they simultaneously howled in laughter. When they finished wiping the tears from their eyes and caught their breath, Blomberg said, "Revenge for what?"

"Two years ago, Ekkrot was arrested for violating the Sex Equality and Dignity Act of 1999. He called his girlfriend 'impractical.'"

Blomberg weighed this. "Maybe he was provoked."

"That's not the point. We know that Salamander sees herself as a gender vigilante."

"What about Arssen? How does he fit in?"

"Three years ago he was convicted on two counts of crimes against coital parity."

"What did he do?"

"Apparently he met some woman in a bar in Östermalm and brought her back to his apartment. She got into bed while Arssen took a quick shower, shaved, and brushed his teeth. By the time he climbed under the covers, she was already drowsy. But they had sex anyway. Twice, in fact."

Blomberg whistled.

"That's not the end of it. Six months later, he was charged with criminal negligence involving a method of birth control. He was spending the night with a girl he'd apparently known for some years. She was helping him slip on a condom when he climaxed all over her hand. He claimed that it was a case of premature ejaculation, but the woman said it was intentional. The judge accepted her story."

Blomberg pondered the fact that Arssen's father had mentioned nothing about his son's two convictions. Still, Blomberg couldn't fully believe that Salamander had murdered both Arssen and the author of *The Life Cycle of the Baltic Sturgeon, with Particular Attention to Matters of Coastline Breeding*. The book had made a profound impression on Blomberg as a boy; indeed, its magnificent descriptive passages of the fish's toothless mouth inspired him to become a writer.

"Let's agree these guys did some pretty sordid things," Blomberg said. "The same could be said for many men, and not just Swedes—also Norwegians and even Danes. Why target these two?"

"That's what we have to figure out," Bubbles said. "We've established that two months ago Arssen called Ekkrot on his cell phone."

"They knew each other."

"Cell phone records show they talked half a dozen times. We don't know if they ever met. But they did speak. Once for close to two hours."

Blomberg drew a deep breath. *Lizzy, what kind of trouble have you gotten yourself into this time?* A voice appeared to hack into his brain: "None of your fucking business, Kalle Fucking Blomberg."

"Okay, Mikael," Bubbles said. "I kept up my side of the bargain. I showed you our principal piece of evidence in an ongoing investigation. Now tell me what you've got."

Blomberg drew a deep breath. Then he held a comb over his upper lip and stuck out his hand in a stiff-armed salute.

"Must we always play charades?" Bubbles asked.

It was an arrangement that the two had worked out. Blomberg didn't feel as bad about revealing information obtained through confidential sources, as long as the inspector was forced to guess.

Blomberg continued to hold the comb before his upper lip and extend his arm stiffly.

"Mustache," said Bubbles. "Nazi salute."

Blomberg nodded encouragingly.

"Hitler."

Blomberg smile broadly. He next pointed at the desk in Bubbles's office.

"Self-assembled . . . four-legged . . . UKEA!"

Blomberg next pretended to sketch the desk. Then to type on an imaginary keyboard.

Bubbles wrinkled his brow. "Arssen was writing a thriller that claimed UKEA's early models were based on designs by Hitler?"

Blomberg nodded passionately.

"Who on earth told you this?"

"C'mon, Svenjamin, you know I can't reveal that."

"Have you read Arssen's manuscript?"

"That's the problem. It disappeared at the time of his murder. No one knows where it is."

"So you think Arssen was murdered to stop him from blowing the whistle on UKEA?"

"I don't know what to think," Blomberg said, "especially after watching that video."

"You really can't imagine Salamander killing a man?"

"Of course I can. Just not a loser like Arssen."

As he was leaving the police station, Blomberg made fleeting eye contact with a female officer. He recognized her immediately. It was Hedda Aas, a former Uppland debutante who'd recently entered the force. Aas was staring at his paunch lasciviously. Blomberg flashed her a coffee- and tobacco-stained smile. The former debutante moaned. She summoned him with a crooked forefinger. Blomberg obediently approached the stunning blond who stood half a head taller than him.

"Are you Mikael Blomberg?"

"I am."

"You're under arrest." The stunning officer moistened her lips.

"But why?" he asked.

"For making me criminally horny."

The officer handcuffed him and led him off to a solitary cell.

FIVE

LÖRDAG, JANUARI 22–TORSDAG, JANUARI 27

84% of Swedish adults describe themselves as atheists; within this group 78% express a strong belief in the existence of trolls.
—ROYAL STATISTICAL ABSTRACT FOR SWEDEN, WITH PARTICULAR
ATTENTION TO THE NORRBOTTEN TUNDRA, 1310–2010

Blomberg sat in Muggen on Götgatan, a kaffebar popular with Väckelsång's poets and conceptual artists. He sipped a vat of Midsommar Murders Dry Roast. Since last seeing Salamander two years ago, Blomberg had periodically tried to contact her, but never with any success. She'd always been elusive, but during this time became only more so. On Facebook, though, Blomberg had come across the following profile:

SEX: Female, generally speaking
BIRTHDAY: Walpurgis Night (read *Faust*, moron)
RELATIONSHIP STATUS: Don't even try
PREFER: Boys, as long as they don't play with my nipples during sex; chicks, too, if they're buff

EMPLOYER: Self
COLLEGE: None
HIGH SCHOOL: Saint Edmundsson's Psychiatric Hospital
NETWORKS: Rage Against Global Patriarchy, support group
cofacilitator
LIKES AND INTERESTS: pi
FAVORITE QUOTATION: Prepare to Die, Motherfucker

MUSIC:
Carnage Collector
Harmonic Bloodbath
Angel Gorefest
Amy Winehouse

TELEVISION:
The Wire
Curb Your Enthusiasm
Sweden's Most Wanted

MOVIES:
The Matrix Reloaded
Shaun of the Dead
The Seventh Seal

BOOKS:
Statistical Field Theory: An Introduction to Exactly Solved Models in Statistical Physics by G. Mussardo
Cosmology in Gauge Field Theory and String Theory by D. Bailin and Alexander Love

An Anthropologist on Mars by Oliver Sacks
The Vices by Lawrence Douglas

FRIENDS: Not applicable

PHOTOS: None

POKE: At your own risk

Was it Salamander's profile? There was no way to be certain, but Blomberg thought he remembered seeing her read *Cosmology in Gauge Field Theory and String Theory* by Bailin and Love while recovering from gunshot wounds to the brain. Or had that been *Neutrinos in Particle Physics, Astronomy, and Cosmology* by Xing and Zhou? He couldn't quite recall. Still, the suspicion lingered.

He felt the powerful need to get in touch with Salamander, if for no other reason than to hear her side of the story. He knew, of course, that it was futile to search for her. Long ago, he'd learned that the best way to reach her was to wait for her to hack into his computer and read his personal files.

Blomberg booted up his computer and named a new file: "Top Ten Rapists on the Swedish National Soccer Team." That was sure to attract Salamander's attention. Then he wrote:

Dear Lizzy, Long time no hear. I've been up to this and that, keeping myself busy. How about you? Kickboxing? Do you still like to wear black? :) On a more serious note, I heard that you recently decapitated and mutilated two guys. One of them was an acquaintance of mine from university days, not that we were particularly close. To be honest, he couldn't write his way out of a Twinkie bag. :-(Anyway Lizzy, I'm not here to judge. I just want to talk. You're in deep trouble and I think I can help. So I do hope you hack into my computer and drop me a note. xx Mikael

The next morning Blomberg noticed something amiss with his computer. His desktop was empty and his entire hard drive had been core dumped. Years ago Salamander had tried to convince him to back up all his work, but somehow he'd always been too lazy. At heart he was a Luddite. Now he registered mild horror that twenty-five years of work had just vanished from his life.

Only one file remained: "Top ELEVEN Rapists on the Swedish National Soccer Team." He tried to open the file but now it was password secured. *Damn you, Lizzy.* He tried the passwords that had worked in the past—Father Flambé, $e^{\pi i}+1$, Back to Black—but nothing worked. He sat in front of his computer for hours, smoking, drinking mugfuls of Colombian Pyroclastic Dark Roast, and pounding in password after password. Finally he tried typing in his name. The file promptly opened. The note wasn't long.

Dear Kalle Fucking Blomberg (yes, I know about the liberal dowager queen Hedvig Eleonora of Holstein-Gottorp),
I don't need your fucking help. >:(
Lizzy S.
PS: I still wear black.
PPS: I uploaded your hard drive to an account on Sverigemail .com. You really must learn to back up all your work. It's not too late, even for a fat old warthog like you.

Fat old warthog? Instinctively Blomberg sucked in his gut. *Must cut back on the fried eel.*

He hoped Salamander would get back in touch with him, but another day passed without any further communication. She'd probably fled to Eritrea to avoid arrest, but he found himself walking in the direction of her apartment on Svartensgatan anyway. Blomberg was the only other person in the world who knew the location of the apartment. It was −47 degrees with a brisk 70 km/h wind coming off the Baltic. Blomberg turned up the collar of his coat and thrust his hands in his pockets. Two years ago, when he'd helped Salamander settle some of the legal issues associated with stapling her half brother to a warehouse ceiling, Blomberg had figured out the security code to her apartment. He suspected that she hadn't bothered to change it. Carefully he punched in:

3.14159265358979323846264338327950288419716939937510582097494459230781640628620899862803482534211706798214808651328230664709384460955058223172535940812848111745028410270193852110555964462294895493038196442881097566593344612847564823378678316527120190914564856692346034861045432664821339360726024914127372458700660631558817488152092096282925409171536436789259036001133053054882046652138414695194151160

and let himself in through the front door.

The apartment was over 3,800 square feet, with a 73-square-foot balcony and a 221-square-foot sundeck. Nineteen of the twenty-one rooms in the flat were completely unfurnished. Salamander preferred a minimalist aesthetic. Not that she appeared to spend a lot of time at home. A layer of dust covered the floor. The Poggen-pohl kitchen was stocked with the latest appliances, but none showed any sign of use. Next to the sink was a four-foot stack of Big Bill's takeout pizza boxes. Frowning from the smell, Blomberg peered into one box. It contained two half-eaten pepperoni slices covered with green furry mold. *The gal's no domestic goddess.*

He glanced in the Viking refrigerator. It was empty save for a couple of 32-ounce bottles of flat Coke and a box of Twinkies.

Bubbles frowned. *Why refrigerate the Twinkies?*

The bathroom told much the same story. Cigarette ashes covered the tub and bidet. Three bottles of eyeliner and eye shadow stood in the medicine cabinet. Blomberg examined the labels. Dr. Hauschka's Death Black.

The bed showed no signs of having recently been slept in. On her nightstand was the same novel that had appeared on the Facebook page: *The Vices* by Lawrence Douglas.

Must order it on Amazon, thought Blomberg.

Also on her nightstand was a framed photograph. To Blomberg's surprise, it appeared to be a photo of Salamander's family taken when Lizzy was no more than five. There was a smiling redheaded Lizzy and her blond twin sister, Chamelea. The two sisters flanked their father, Dmitri Kalashnikov, the former KGB agent who, in the years before being lit on fire and axed in the head by his daughter, had been quite handsome. Presumably the mother had taken the picture. *Säg omelett!* Say omelet! The photo spoke of happier times, before a pattern of physical abuse, murderous assaults, and attempted live burials had strained family ties.

Deep down she's just a little girl who's still hurting from Daddy's rejection.

"Cut the amateur psychologizing, Kalle Fucking Blomberg."

At times Salamander's voice made itself present in Blomberg's mind with such sharpness that it scared him. Accustomed to her hacking into his computer, he felt that she had also succeeded in hacking directly into his brain. *Impossible. Must tell my therapist on Tuesday.*

The emptiness of the flat made Blomberg uncomfortable. A long corridor opened onto one vacant room after another. At last Blomberg found the door to Salamander's study. Here he found a pair of night-vision goggles, a hunting knife, some rope and tape, an ATFLIR infrared targeting system, a handful of FIM-92 Stinger surface-to-air missiles, several thermobaric BLU-118/B laser-guided bunker busters, an unopened CBU-97 Sensor Fuzed Weapon, and a new AH-64D Apache Longbow combat helicopter that Salamander appeared to have assembled herself. And of course there was her thirty-foot-long eight-ton Tera 10 mainframe supercomputer.

Blomberg sat in her Stressless chair and sighed. *Ah, Lizzy.*

He was about to try his hand at her computer when he noticed a small printed notice next to the keyboard: "Unauthorized accessing of this computer will result in the destruction of all life-forms within a 3km radius." A number of colorful wires ran from the mainframe to the ordnance scattered haphazardly around the study. For an Asperger's-like savant, Salamander could be an awful slob. Blomberg decided not to test his luck.

Inspector Bubbles pulled back the sheet. The reindeer had been bound, trussed, and eviscerated, with a latex mask pulled over its face. It was turning into a very bad month. First the two decapitations, and now the Reindeer Killer had struck again. At least he had a suspect in the decapitations. The reindeer were turning into a bigger nightmare. The headlines of the *Aftonbladet* screamed: THIRD REINDEER SLAIN: BUBBLES BAFFLED.

"Have you ever seen anything like this before?" Bubbles asked.

"I've seen my fair share of killed reindeer." The answer came from Professor Dr. Sven Svenssen, chief of Reindeer Forensics at the Royal Pathological Institute. Bubbles usually preferred to keep investigations within the force, but in the last days he became convinced of the need to work with the Institute. Not that it made him happy. He found the researchers at the Institute arrogant, particularly the guys in Reindeer.

"That's not what I asked," said Bubbles. "I mean, have you ever seen a killing quite like this?"

"No, perhaps not *exactly* like this."

Why was it always such a pain getting a straight answer from the guys in Reindeer?

"Have you ascertained a cause of death?"

"Strangulation." Professor Dr. Svenssen showed Bubbles the marks on the throat of the reindeer. "Obviously the killer is extremely strong. It is exceptionally difficult to strangle a reindeer with bare hands."

Bubbles nodded. *Oh, really? I thought strangling a five hundred-kilogram mammal was like picking wild strawberries.*

"Judging by the handprint on the neck, I would say your killer is rather large. Approximately seven feet tall and upwards of three hundred pounds."

Bubbles wrote "rather large??" in a notebook.

"Any signs of sexual molestation?"

"I'll have to do more tests, but I see no indications of penetration, which we saw in the case of the Reindeer Defiler of 1998. Of course, this time the animal has been completely disemboweled."

"The disemboweling occurred after the strangling?"

"That would be my conclusion, yes."

"Why would a killer disembowel his dead victim?"

"It's hard to say. The Reindeer Disemboweler of 1992 did it out of rage against his father, who was a very successful taxidermist in Norrbottens Iän but apparently a rather distant and judgmental parent. Altogether different was the case of the Reindeer Ripper of 1986. He acted out of what we call organ lust, a near sexual need for reindeer innards. I explained this all to your colleague."

Blomberg glanced at Professor Dr. Svenssen. "Colleague? What colleague?"

"The private investigator. Jane Manhater."

"Did you say Manhater?"

"Yes. I assumed you knew her."

"Well, sure, I know her, but it's been some time. I'm trying to remember . . . *Rather* short, I recall, under five feet, right? With death-black hair?"

"Actually I think it's dyed. I believe she's a natural redhead. Like Pippi Longstocking."

Just then Bubbles noticed the bandage across Professor Dr. Svenssen's nose, his two black eyes, and the sloppy tattoo on his forehead. *OINK!*

"By any chance do you know where I could find Fröken Manhater?"

"She's been staying at my little lakeside cottage up in Smörgås-bord. Should I tell her to give you a call?"

"No, no, don't bother. I'll get in touch with her."

Erotikka peeled off her blouse and slipped out of her bra.

"Boo and Baa have come out to play." She placed her hand on the crotch of Blomberg's jeans. "Does Stiggi want to come out and play with Boo and Baa?"

"Stiggi's a bit . . . fatigued," Blomberg said.

"Fatigued?" Erotikka pouted, tugging on Blomberg's belt. "Maybe Stiggi needs some mouth-to-mouth resuscitation."

"Maybe a little later, dear."

"No," Erotikka said decisively. "Stiggi must entertain his friends. Boo and Baa don't like to play alone."

Blomberg sighed as Erotikka removed his clothes.

Twenty minutes later she lay curled on her side, arm slung across Blomberg's belly. "I don't know what it is about you. Here I am, a forty-five-year-old woman, and you make me feel like a—"

"Yes, dear. I know. A reindeer in rut."

Abruptly Erotikka sat up in bed. "Okay, tell me what's bothering you."

Blomberg shrugged.

"It's that business with Salamander, isn't it?"

"I just don't get it," Blomberg said. "Arssen's father is convinced that Twig was killed because he was going to blow the whistle on UKEA's connection with Hitler. And I know for a fact that UKEA has done its best to remove all the Hitler sketches from its archive of early table and bookcase designs. But Bubbles is convinced that

Salamander is the killer, that she acted alone as a vigilante, decapitating both Ekkrot and Arssen in order to exact vengeance against two sleazes of patriarchy."

"You don't buy that?"

"It just doesn't make sense. If Lizzy wanted to rid Sweden of all its violent misogynists, why start with these two? These guys were total small fry in the world of gender hegemony."

"Maybe she didn't like their writing."

"I thought about that, too. But everybody loves *The Life Cycle of the Baltic Sturgeon, with Particular Attention to Matters of Coastline Breeding.* I'm not even convinced she has ever read Ekkrot's books. Salamander's tastes in readings are quite limited. Relativistic space cosmology, that kind of thing. And there's no reason to believe that she ever read a word by Twig. The guy never published."

"So you think Bubbles is wrong?"

"It just seems completely crazy. But I saw the video, Erotikka. It's definitely Salamander. The way she lops off the head. The way she lines up the penalty shot and kicks the head, it's just so Lizzy. Only it doesn't add up."

"Have you tried contacting her?"

"It's useless. She's completely vanished. And Bubbles thinks he's going to find her. What a joke. It will be a toasty day in Lapland before the police ever track her down. I'm afraid she's gone for good."

Just then Ralf, Erotikka's husband, stirred from his corner of the bed. "I couldn't help but overhear your conversation," he said.

"Ralfie, what did I say about eavesdropping?" Erotikka said sternly.

"I'm sorry, but I thought you guys should take a look at this."

He handed Blomberg his iPad 3G with built-in 802.11n Wi-Fi. It was opened to the banner headline of the *Svenska Dagbladet*.

SALAMANDER SEIZED BY POLICE IN DAWN RAID AT REINDEER PATHOLOGIST'S LAKESIDE SHÅGSHÄCK; INSPECTOR BUBBLES CONFIRMS ARREST; SWEDEN'S MOST DANGEROUS WOMAN UNDER FIVE FEET CHARGED IN DOUBLE HOMICIDE.

"Impossible," Blomberg muttered.

SIX

FREDAG, JANUARI 28–MÅNDAG, JANUARI 31

The construction of sub-basement sex dungeons in suburban
Stockholm jumped by over 16% in the past decade.
—"SLAVES IN SUBURBIA: A GROWING SOCIAL PROBLEM?"
REPORT OF THE MUNICIPAL TASK FORCE ON SEXUAL
PERVERSITY IN SWEDISH COMMUTER COMMUNITIES
(STOCKHOLM, UPPSALA, AND GÖTEBORG), MARCH 2008

Officer Snorkkle stared at the detainee through a narrow slit in the titanium reinforced door of her solitary cell.

"Cold enough?" he asked with a laugh. "Cunt."

Salamander folded her arms to keep warm. It was –34 degrees in the cell. She wore black jeans and a black tank top.

"You are sooooooo screwed," Snorkkle whispered.

Salamander didn't answer.

"Let's see you try to hack your skanky little snatch out of an isolation cell," Snorkkle chortled.

Salamander jogged in place to generate body heat.

"Little hacker ho finding it hard to adjust to life in solitary?" He laughed maliciously.

Just then Snorkkle heard the buzzer on the outer door to the detention unit. Before him stood a young man in a Big Bill's Pizza jumpsuit. "I have a special delivery for Lizzy Salamander. One large pie with extra pepperoni and cheese."

Officer Snorkkle searched his pocket to tip the deliveryman.

"No sweat, Officer. It's all been paid in advance. Paypal."

An hour later, a UPS truck arrived at the detention facility. "I have three boxes for Lizzy Salamander."

Officer Snorkkle helped the deliverywoman carry the boxes into the solitary cell.

Some time later, the FedEx truck arrived.

Officer Snorkkle peered into the cell. Salamander was now seated in a comfortable recliner, reading *Mathematical Principles of Signal Processing: Fourier and Wavelet Analysis* by Pierre Brémaud. Around her legs was tucked a fluffy black mohair throw. She was nibbling on pizza crust and sipping espresso.

"Your days are soooooo numbered," seethed Snorkkle. Some minutes later he said politely, "Could I have one slice?"

Salamander gave him the finger without looking up from her book.

Since her arrest, Salamander had refused to speak to the police. Inspectors Flunk and Snorkkle had managed only to get bitten on their foreheads.

After her second day of detention, Chief Inspector Bubbles entered Salamander's isolation cell and stood akimbo. Without saying a word, he opened a portable chess set and placed it on the UKEA coffee table that Salamander had assembled that morning. Bubbles finished arranging the pieces.

"If you win, no questions. If I win, we get to interrogate you. Deal?"

Imperceptibly she nodded.

"Is it okay if I play black?" she said in a near whisper.

"Whatever you prefer."

Bubbles adjusted the old Soviet time clock. They each got two hours for their first forty moves.

The first game ended in a draw. As did the second, third, and fourth.

"You're pretty good," Salamander said grudgingly.

"You're not bad yourself," said the inspector.

The next morning Bubbles reappeared in Salamander's cell. Without a word of greeting, he gruffly asked, "What's special about 162?"

Salamander answered promptly. "It's the smallest number that can be written as the sum of four positive squares in nine ways."

Bubbles barely nodded.

Then Salamander fired off a question of her own. "How about 164, copper?"

"It's the smallest number that's a concatenation of squares in two different ways," said the inspector.

Salamander shivered ever so vaguely.

"183?" Bubbles said.

"Smallest number n so that n concatenated with n+1 is square!" cried Salamander. "187?"

"Smallest quasi-Charmichael number in base 7!" shouted Bubbles. "210?"

"Product of first four primes!"

". . . 9415?"

"Sum of first nineteen numbers that have digit sum nineteen!"

"9856?"

"Number of ways to place two nonattacking knights on a twelve-by-twelve chessboard!"

They fell back in their chairs sweaty and exhausted. Salamander blew a strand of death-black hair that had fallen across her brow. "That was . . . good," she said, barely above a whisper.

Blomberg adjusted his tie and hair. "I'll be back," he said.

"Hey, flat-chested hacker ho," Officer Snorkkle snarled. "You have a visitor."

Salamander found herself unexpectedly hurt by Snorkkle's insults. The year before she'd flown to New York to have her boobs done by a world-famous plastic surgeon on Long Island. She hadn't wanted anything extravagant; she just wanted breasts larger than those of her fourteen-year-old nephew. The surgeon thought she should at least enlarge them to 32 AAA, but Salamander didn't want to look buxom. Now she regretted not following the surgeon's advice.

"Hey, cyber-cunt. Did you hear me? Some loser is here to visit you."

Salamander made herself a mental note. *One day I must char off Snorkkle's testicles.*

She was brought to the visitors' room. The first thing she saw was the familiar monogrammed briefcase, KFB.

Kalle Fucking Blomquvist. Or whatever his name is now.

"Hello, Lizzy."

"Hello, Blomstein."

"—berg."

"Whatever."

"You know, I discovered that my family was formerly Jewish."

"Spare me the lecture about the liberal reign of dowager queen Hedvig Eleonora of Holstein-Gottorp."

Blomberg remembered with a smile that she had learned about his ancestors when she'd hacked into his computer and erased his entire hard drive. It had been two years since they'd last seen each other. A lot had changed in those two years. Volvo had been sold to China. Saab had been declared dead, only to be rescued at the last minute by the Dutch. Three new coffee bars had opened in Stockholm.

Blomberg thought the years stood Salamander well. Always petite, she had filled out. "You've gained a few grams," he said.

Suddenly she reached out and grabbed a fistful of his gut. "And what do you call this?" she hissed.

Blomberg doubled over in pain. "I meant it as a compliment, Lizzy. You look good. And I like your T-shirt."

It was sleeveless and black. It said: DO I LOOK LIKE A FUCKING PEOPLE PERSON?

"I don't feel good," she said.

"What's bothering you?" *The fact that you're in a maximum security holding cell charged with two heinous murders?*

She shrugged. "I don't know. I'm turning thirty."

Blomberg's eyes teared up with nostalgia. Lizzy turning thirty! She'd been a boyish twenty-five when they'd had sex in the dungeon of one of Sweden's leading titans of industry/psychopathic killers.

They strolled over to the prison Starbucks, popular with the

Jämtland gangbangers. Blomberg watched her deposit four heaping teaspoons of sugar into her coffee. Not everything had changed.

"How's your family?" Blomberg asked.

"All dead."

"Your sister?"

"For all intents and purposes."

Blomberg smiled. He thought about the photo in Salamander's apartment, the two sisters, the one redheaded, the other blond. He glanced at the red roots peeking through her death-black hair.

"Has anyone ever told you that if you let your natural hair grow out," Blomberg said, "you'd be a dead ringer for Pippi Long-stocking?"

Salamander snorted. "Yeah, like everyone, duh. Anyway, I'm sick of hearing about that loser. Pippi let her father do unspeakable things to her anus."

"Really? I don't recall that."

"I suggest you reread *Pippi and the Oxelösund Shågshäck.*"

"I don't think my mother read me that one."

"It was the last in the series." Salamander stared glumly at the floor. She let a string of drool fall from her lips and then sucked it back into her mouth.

"I wish you wouldn't do that."

She lit a cigarette and blew smoke straight in his face.

"Nor that. Look, Lizzy, I'm here to help you."

"I don't need your help, Kalle Fucking Blomski."

"—berg. And my first name is Mikael. *And* I happen to have a *real* middle name. It's Solomon."

"Kalle Fucking Bloomski," she repeated.

"You've murdered two men, Lizzy. I'm not here to judge. I

know you've had some anger management issues over the years. But you need a good advokat. There are still plenty of prosecutors and police who feel you got off scot-free for axing your father's head in two, stapling your half brother to the ceiling, hanging your legal guardian upside down by a fishhook, and turning a gang of bikers into eunuchs."

Even Lizzy had to acknowledge that she had a complicated legal history. And as if to underscore Blomberg's concern, Officer Snorkkle walked past them, silently mouthing the words "This time we're going to nail your satanic cunt to the wall, you sick transgender bitch."

"I was proven innocent," Salamander said. "Remember?"

"That was then, Lizzy. This is now. Prosecutors are looking at a double homicide. With bodily mutilation. And surgical decapitation. They're going to throw the book at you. This is Sweden, Lizzy, not Iceland. You could go to prison for five years. Possibly six."

"I didn't do it. Why would I waste my time killing an unpublished thriller writer?"

"You know as well as I do that Arssen was convicted of two counts of semi-consensual intercourse with a drowsy woman."

"So he deserved to die. It doesn't mean that I did it."

"Lizzie, I saw the tape."

"What tapc?"

"The whole thing was captured on CCTV. Milksop, your old employer, installed several surveillance cameras in Arssen's apartment two weeks before he was decapitated."

"I'm surprised they didn't hire me freelance to do the job." Salamander sounded vaguely offended.

"I've seen the video. The images are sharp. And it's you, Lizzy, cutting off the head and kicking it across the living room. It's your sword, your moves, your soccer kick."

"Only it wasn't me." She fixed her death-black eyes on Blomberg in her I'm-telling-the-fucking-truth stare.

"Can you prove it?"

"I'll need my computer."

Blomberg thought this over. "I'll see what I can do."

"And Blomsky, a box of Twinkies wouldn't hurt."

As Blomberg was leaving the gaol, he noticed a female guard eying his paunch. Her name was Mirka Määttä. Määttä stood half a head taller than Blomberg. A pair of perfect breasts was tearing tiny holes through her skintight yellow and blue police tank top. Before joining the force, Määttä had been a jet-setting supermodel but decided she wanted to contribute more to Swedish society.

"I suppose you're going to say that I make you unspeakably horny," he said, flashing her his receding gums.

The guard stuffed her police-issue thong in his mouth. She grabbed him by the tie and pulled him into a special interrogation cell.

Smuggling Salamander's eight-ton Tera 10 mainframe supercomputer into her cramped prison cell was more complicated than Blomberg had anticipated. Fortunately Blomberg still had a contact at Posten AB from a piece he had done on extortion, gang rape, and money laundering in the Swedish overnight delivery business. The contact, an ethnic Estonian with a Latvian granduncle, was able to "borrow" a truck from the Royal Postal Agency. He packed the mainframe into thirty Viking refrigerator boxes.

Salamander claimed she needed the refrigerators for her Twinkies. Since her arrest, she'd gone on a hunger strike, eating nothing but pepperoni and extra cheese pizza. Finally Inspector Bubbles had relented and permitted her to receive a shipment of two thousand boxes of Twinkies. But a guard's suspicions were aroused when the Royal Postal Agency truck arrived with the thirty "refrigerators."

"Since when do Twinkies need to be refrigerated?" asked the guard.

The Estonian broke into a cold sweat, but was quick on his feet. "The fridges aren't meant to keep the Twinkies cold. The detainee feared that if the Twinkies were left out in boxes, mice would get to them."

The guard looked at him closely, then waved him through.

Securing a reliable power source for the Tera 10 proved another headache. The single three-pronged outlet in Salamander's cell was far from adequate. Blomberg learned that Vattenfall had recently constructed a 90 megawatt wind farm three miles from the gaol. With help of his Estonian friend, Blomberg was able to run heavy-duty cables from the wind farm to Salamander's cell. The hookup caused a minor brownout in Western Svealand, but Blomberg used his blog to blame this on uncharacteristically windless weather.

Once the computer was up and running, Blomberg paid Salamander a fresh visit in her cell.

"Let's check out this video," said Salamander.

The police had stored the file in its Cray X2 "Black Widow," reserved for its most ultrasensitive evidence. The files were protected behind SonicWALL's E-Class NSA 7500 firewall, the most impregnable in the world.

It took Salamander twenty seconds to hack in.

"How on earth do you do that?" Blomberg asked.

"I designed the system and its security protocols."

"I see."

Blomberg slurped coffee and Salamander snacked on Twinkies as they watched the video.

"It's you, Lizzy."

"False." Her eyes narrowed in serpentine fury. "Look carefully, Kalle Fucking Blomwitz."

"—berg."

He studied the film. The assailant certainly looked a whole lot like Lizzy, down to the death-black lipstick.

"The T-shirt, Kalle, study the tee."

He did. It was black. On it was Tweety Bird firing an M16. *Prepare to die, Puddy Fucking Cat!*

"So?"

"Are you blind? I don't own that T-shirt! I fucking *hate* yellow canaries."

So Tweety Bird is a canary. Somehow Blomberg had never made the connection. Still, what did that prove?

"I'll talk to Bubbles," he said, "but I'm not confident that that's going to convince him to drop the charges. Anything else?"

"Look here."

Blomberg watched as the assailant waved her samurai sword in a crazy display of murderous virtuosity.

"I'm looking . . ."

"I'm a lefty, Mr. Observant."

It was true that the warrior carried her sword in her right hand. "Worthy of attention," Blomberg conceded. "But hardly dispositive. Anything else?"

Next Salamander froze a frame and blew up the image. It was the moment just after the assailant had nimbly trotted up the walls and across the ceiling and was about to deliver the lethal swing of the sword to her victim. In that instant, the assailant's neck was extended forward, revealing part of a tattoo.

"So?"

"The tattoo. Look closely."

Blomberg leaned forward. "It appears to be a ... fish ... maybe a sturgeon."

"A Baltic sturgeon, to be exact," Salamander said.

As if reading Blomberg's thoughts, Salamander bent over, tossing her hair forward, exposing her neck. Peeking over her Burton hoodie was the familiar head of a Tyrannosaurus chewing on a leg of a velociraptor.

"See, no new tattoos," she said. "Just the same old Zallinger mural."

Blomberg remembered the time five years ago when he'd first seen Salamander naked. She'd been an energetic but unexpectedly shy lover. And she'd complained about the tattoo that covered most of her back. "I should get it redone. Zallinger's work was produced at a time when dinosaurs were still considered reptilian and lugubrious. In the mural, the Tyrannosaurus is dragging his tail. Paleontologists now believe that the tail would have been held in the air, to counterpoise his body weight as he bounded after his prey. The dude was no slowpoke."

"Maybe you used makeup to cover over the *T. rex* and used a temporary tattoo of a Baltic sturgeon," Blomberg said.

"Right," said Salamander. "Only look here."

One advantage of having the most powerful computer in continental Europe in her holding cell was that Salamander was able to blow up the images with extraordinary resolution. She focused in on the back of the assailant's neck. Blomberg could clearly make out the pores of the assailant's skin and the individual skin pricks that had made the sturgeon tattoo. The tattoo was bona fide. And he could also clearly see the roots of the assailant's death-black hair. Which happened to be blond.

"Well, if the girl with the sturgeon tattoo isn't you," he said, "who is it?"

Salamander smiled her crooked nonsmile. "I have a pretty good idea."

She stood in the clearing by the wood. It was approximately 150,000 square feet, maybe a little larger now that the beaver family had taken down the Douglas fir by the brook. The lichen tasted good for this time of year. Not as good as November lichen, which was sweet and mossy, but much better than August lichen, which was dry and flavorless. Her lips were a bit sore from nibbling at the permafrost and her fourth stomach growled: She should have known better than to eat those moldy leaves after breakfast. At least her antlers were feeling less sore. They'd been aching since her argument with Partner. It was the first time they'd come to blows, and now both were still nervous around each other. She couldn't even remember what they'd argued about. *I can't even remember when Junior was born. Truth be told, I have no memories whatsoever. Everything is just one continuous present. It sucks being a reindeer.*

At least she knew the days were already getting longer. Soon she'd be in heat. Then she'd have to put up with Partner. He was a handsome bull with an impressive rack. Gray whiskers had begun to sprout around his chin, but his nostrils were still fabulous, and she never tired of his rutting cry: *AGGGGGWWRRHHH-HHH.*

Nonetheless.

She stole a glance at Partner. There he was urinating directly on the nice lichen. Had he always done that? Where had he picked up such behavior? When nature called, she liked to go in a stand of birch trees. But he didn't seem to care. Nor did he seem to mind that he'd just peed directly on his lunch. No, he just kept nibbling away at the steaming lichen. *A real pig.*

All at once she began to dread mating season. She didn't mind being mounted, but not in the middle of a meal or while she was trying to sleep or when Junior was watching. But Partner paid no heed. Sometimes she suspected that he did that on purpose, just to humiliate her. He just climbed on, day or night, rain or shine, did his business, wham bam, thank you, ma'am—except not even a thank-you. Just a grunt and he was back to nibbling on urine-stained lichen. Her pleasure didn't compute. All she was left with was a crazy backache from having to bear his weight. *Really no different than a wild boar.*

Maybe all bulls are the same. Generally speaking, he served as a good role model for Junior, showing him how to peel moss from tree trunks with his antlers. Not that Junior had much in that department yet. Junior . . . where exactly was he? She peered around. Where had she last seen him? *Having no memory sucks.*

Suddenly she froze. Who broke that twig? Not Partner. He was still munching on lichen à la urine. And certainly not Junior. His step was far lighter. She twisted her ears. She saw a shadow move between two evergreens. *WTF.* She'd never seen a bear, but knew instinctively that that wasn't one. And wolves don't walk on their hind legs and carry long shiny hunting knives. She caught another glimpse of the creature that wasn't a bear and wasn't a wolf. It was rather tall, with blond head fur and no antlers. Frantically she looked for Junior, but he was nowhere to be seen. The creature leaped out from behind a spruce and was running toward her. Partner nibbled at the lichen, oblivious. Giant paws grabbed her throat. She tried to scream, only to realize that female reindeer make no sounds.

No sooner had Blomberg left her detention cell than Salamander emailed Bubonic, a fellow hackstar. Morbidly obese, chronically unwashed, and clinically paranoid, Bubonic had been Salamander's fuck buddy a few years back. From his unheated windowless 63-square-foot basement apartment, he recently had launched a cyberattack on Europe's and America's largest banking institutions, triggering a flash crash of the all the major markets and a brief worldwide depression.

Salamander typed:

<Yo. Bubonic.>
<Manhater. Long time no chatter. What u been up 2?>
<sort of a long story. we'll catch up later. i have a favor to ask. i just sent a video as an mpeg attachment>
<got it. lol. shows you decapitating some dude. nice work. vintage manhater.>

<thanx, but actually it's not me. study carefully.>

<gotcha. girl in vid has different tattoo. looks like a Baltic sturgeon.>

<quick study. now comes the favor. was hoping you might be able to do some creative work with the vid, like editing out images of the girl and splicing in someone else.>

<anyone in mind?>

<use your imagination.>

<will do. booting up my green screen as we chat.>

The man carefully cut open the chest cavity and removed all the organs. They steamed in the Arctic air. He considered eating the raw heart, but decided against it. Liver tasted better. Then he plunged his hands into the warm cavity and felt around. Nothing. *Scheisse,* he whispered. Then he moved over to the larger one, ate another liver, and felt around. Again nothing. *Double scheisse.* Then he tried the small one. Again zilch. *Scheisse times three.* He toweled his hands off with his monogrammed handkerchief. *PK:* Psychopathic Killer. The hankie was a gift from his deceased twin brother. He noticed, though, that his hands were covered with fresh blood. It took him a minute to figure out where the blood was coming from. Apparently he had accidentally sliced his pinkie off in disemboweling the reindeer. *Crap!* It was the third finger he had accidentally chopped off in as many attacks. Now he had to locate the friggin' pinkie so the cops didn't find it. He'd reattached the last one with Krazy Glue, only to watch it fall off after a couple of weeks. Lousy Krazy Glue! He got down on all fours and began searching. When he next looked up, it was dusk. *Dusk! Night was falling! When the trolls come out of their caves and dance and make weird scary sounds!* His undies felt damp. *Scheisse squared.* He had peed in his pants. Just then he heard a sound. *Was it a chipmunk or the war cry of Skrymir, the green-haired wart dwarf who feeds on clovers and German giants?*

The seven-fingered monstrosity ran wildly across the frozen field.

Salamander watched the revised video that Bubonic had sent her. She smiled, but not crookedly. This was a big toothsome smile that showed off her improbably perfect teeth. Her father might have been a cold-blooded KGB murderer, but he'd paid for the best orthodontic care in all of Göteborg.

She noticed that Snorkkle was studying her, perplexed. She immediately reset her features in a scowl. Snorkkle moved on.

Promptly she poked Mendax, another cyberbuddy, a super-shadowy figure who floated like a ghost between servers, routers, domain names, and email addresses. A legendary figure among cyberfreaks, web geeks, and netheads, he came into being for nanoseconds at a time, only to dematerialize in a cascading cancel-bot, reappearing moments later on another continent, on another server, in another fleeting domain. Mendax had kept a low profile ever since posting on an open forum classified material that showed how to build a thermonuclear warhead with material available at a corner drugstore. This led to a global manhunt and arrest warrants for unpaid parking tickets in London and outstanding library fines in Berlin. But no one was able to locate Mendax, leading to admiring speculation that he didn't actually exist.

<hi Mendax>
<Manhater. Long time no text>
<Really. What u been up 2?>

<Same old same old. If I told u I'd have to kill u>

<okay, we'll keep it brief then. I have a favor to ask. I've attached a video. Would u know how 2 leak it so it gets maximum exposure?>

<U want me to arrange a leak? Minimax or maximax?>

<Maximax>

<I think I can do that>

<thanx, Mendax. I owe u 1. Look me up if u ever make it 2 sweden>

<OK, but not my first destination. OAO>

Chief Inspector Bubbles and Officers Flunk and Snorkkle examined the bodies of the slaughtered family. The bull appeared to have been strangled and cut open at the point of attack. The female had been bound and trussed like in the last killing. Her mouth had been carved in a macabre smile. The young reindeer had been hung upside down.

Flunk fought back tears. "That little guy couldn't have been much more than a year old."

Bubbles nodded grimly. "Officer, please control your emotions." *A typically Finnish response.*

"Sorry, sir. It's just I can't help thinking about my daughter." Flunk blew his nose. "It could have been her."

"Our killer targets reindeer, Officer."

"Flunk has a point," said Snorkkle. "Who knows who she'll go after next? No one is safe from that skanky ho."

Bubbles glared at Snorkkle. "Officer, you can't possibly think Fröken Salamander is responsible for these murders."

"She's a psycho-cunt."

"Officer, may I remind you that Salamander is presently in gaol surrounded by twenty members of the Swedish Special Forces. Professor Doktor Svenssen has already made it clear that our suspect in these slayings is a rather large male." Snorkkle completely missed Bubbles's ironic use of *rather*.

"She's a witchy cunt. She can do crazy witchy stuff." Snorkkle waved his hands in front of his face, imitating a spell being cast.

C.I. Bubbles drew a deep breath. "If you continue like this, I'm going to remove you from the case."

Snorkkle kept waving his arms, casting a mock spell. "Crazy cunty witchy shit. *Expecto Patronum!*"

"Stop that immediately. You're frightening Flunk."

"Protego Horribilis! Avada Kedavra!!"

Just then something caught Bubbles's eye. From the grass he removed his grisly find and place it in a specimen bag.

Flunk shrieked hysterically. "The witch's finger! She chopped off her own finger!"

"What did I tell you?" Snorkkle said.

"Don't be a fool. Salamander's hands are tiny. Look at the size of this pinkie. It's the killer's. But it doesn't look like it was bitten off by a struggling reindeer. It appears our killer had an accident. *Odd. When was the last time that a reindeer killer accidentally cut off his own finger? Must check the files.*

"She chopped it off!" howled Officer Flunk. "Her own finger!"

Bubbles placed a calming protective arm around the officer's shoulders and led him to their car. Snorkkle continued to cast his mock spells.

SEVEN

TISDAG, FEBRUARI 1–LÖRDAG, FEBRUARI 5

i to π: Be rational.
π to i: Get real.

POLICE RELEASE VIDEO OF SLAYING OF UNPUBLISHED THRILLER WRITER.

It was the lead story of the morning news. Blomberg bolted up in bed as Erotikka worked on reviving Stiggi.

"Quick, Ralf, the sound."

Erotikka's husband fetched the remote and turned up the volume.

The newscaster wore a cable-knit sweater and sipped from a mug of Morning Avalanche Multiroast. "Viewers who haven't finished their breakfast yogurt and muesli may not want to watch this. It contains graphic and upsetting images. According to police, the video is the principal piece of evidence linking Lizzy Salamander, the notorious psychohacker, to the crime. Salamander is currently in police custody."

"Odd," Blomberg said, trying to ignore the distracting work of

Erotikka's hands and mouth. "The police rarely go public with their evidence. Something isn't right."

Ralf nodded in agreement.

Blomberg studied the video closely. It was immediately apparent that it was different from the version he'd seen in Salamander's cell. Arssen's poor head still suffered the same fate. But there was no girl ninja nimbly running upside down across the ceiling, brandishing a rare samurai sword. Or rather, there *was* a girl—only it wasn't Salamander. This one had emerald green eyes, a striking red ponytail braid, and wore a cowboy hat and leather wrangler's chaps. And was animated.

"Jessie!" Ralf exclaimed "The Yodeling Cowgirl from *Toy Story 2*!"

"And *Toy Story 3*," added Blomberg.

"We all knew Jessie was quite excitable," said Ralf. "But murder?"

"I don't buy it." This came from Erotikka, who'd temporarily taken a break from her ministrations to Stiggi. "She's been framed."

"But seriously," said Ralf. "Why on earth would the police do that to their own video?"

"I assume the police didn't have a hand in this," said Blomberg gnomically.

"Then who did?"

Blomberg smiled crookedly. "I have an idea."

"Who, *who, WHO* posted that video?" Chief Inspector Bubbles thundered. Officer Flunk had never seen the chief in such a state. His face turned as red as a herring.

"We don't know, sir."

"Well, find out, damn it! And in the meantime get that video off the net. NOW. We're the laughingstock of Northern Europe."

"We're trying, sir."

"What do you mean, trying?"

"I'm afraid all our computers are down."

"That's impossible."

"It's true, sir. We seem to be under some kind of denial-of-service attack."

"From who?"

"It's cleverly masked. It appears to be coming from every computer on the planet simultaneously."

Bubbles swigged some Pepto-Bismol. *Why didn't I go to work for Volvo? Good benefits, early retirement.*

"Sorry, sir. I've never seen anything quite like this. You better take a look for yourself."

Bubbles sat before a monitor. To his dismay, the screen was unresponsive. It remained blank save for an image of a robotic red eye. All at once the computer spoke: "I'm not feeling like myself, Dave. Would you like to hear me sing a song?"

Without waiting for an answer, the computer began:

> *Daisy, daisy,*
> *Give me your answer, do.*
> *I'm half crazy,*
> *All for the love of you.*

It was badly out of tune. "Make it stop," Bubbles cried.

"We're trying, sir."

It won't be a stylish marriage—
I can't afford a carriage,

"Aren't we supposed to have the most secure computers in the entire fucking country?"

Flunk looked stunned. It was the first time he'd ever heard the chief use the F-word. "We do, sir. Two months ago we just completed a multimillion-kronor upgrade of all the firewalls of our computer system. It was done by Milksop Security, the best outfit in all of Scandinavia."

"Did you say Milksop?"

But you'd look sweet upon the seat
Of a bicycle built for two.

"Yes sir, Milksop. The best there is."

"Who exactly at Milksop handled this FUCKING upgrade?"

"I don't exactly remember, sir. A rather shortish boy, I believe, with black hair. Quite imaginative tattoos. Radovan Armanskov-itzdullah, the head of Milksop—"

"Yes, I know Radovan."

"He vouched that the kid was an absolute computer genius."

Daisy, Daisy,
Give me your answer, do.
I'm half crazy
All for the love of you.

Bubbles retreated to his office and quietly closed the door. He pulled out the file he kept locked in the bottom drawer of his desk.

It was from the Greenland Chamber of Commerce. *Move to Greenland, where sheep outnumber humans ten to one!*

Blomberg received a text message from Salamander.

<Did you see the video on TV?>

<Hard to miss, Lizzy. It was on all the networks. Now it's gone viral on YouTube.>

<Sick.>

<I fear it's just a matter of time before Pixar has it taken down. You've framed Jessie. Buzz isn't going to put up with that.>

<I'm the one who's been framed, KFB. Don't forget that. & the public has a right to know about the quality of police work around here. Anyway, Woody forced Jessie to put his thing in her mouth when they were stuck in that toy box at the end of TS3.>

<Whatever u say. I assume my friend Inspector Bubbles isn't tickled pink w/ u.>

<Yeah, coppers discovered the Tera 10 mainframe. They're in the process of removing it from my cell. All I have left is my iPhone 4 with 960 x 640 pixel resolution.>

<My heart bleeds cold borscht. Now are u going to reveal the identity of the girl w/ the sturgeon tattoo?>

<You're the brilliant investigative journalist, KFB. Get moving.>

Salamander was still sucking wind from her daily Navy SEAL/ special operations exercise program of 100 pull-ups, 200 push-ups, and 300 sit-ups in 90 seconds when she noticed that she'd received an email.

<Listen here, you rancid cunt. You think you can make the Svensk
Polis the butt of the planet and face no consequences? Well,
you're wrong, DEAD wrong. You're going to DIE, you scrawny
slut. You're going to be fucking pitchforked to death. We will tear
out your EVERY nose and eyebrow and belly button and tongue
ring. There is no escaping US. No bodily orifice is safe! You and
that flat chest of yours are *so* dead, you skanky undersize
triple A cyber-ho.
Signed,
The Swedish Society of Psychiatrists, Policemen, Legal Guardians, ex-Soviet spies, and neo-Nazis out to *seriously fuck*
Lizzy Salamander>

Salamander composed a short response.

<Dear Officer Snorkkle,
If you're going to send an anonymous threat by email, I suggest next time you not use your actual email address. I'd be
happy to show you how to set up a dummy email account to
hide your identity. But you'll have to return my mainframe to
my cell.
Best,
Lizzy>

The answer arrived presently.

<I don't know what you're talking about, you rancid little cunt.
Why would I want to threaten a flat-chested loser ho like you?
—Officer Snorkkle (Nemo)>

<Dear Nemo,

Here's a helpful site:

How to Create a Fake Disposable Email Address in Yahoo! That Sends Email to Your Primary Yahoo! Account | eHow.com http://www.ehow.com/how_4834948_sends-email-primary-yahoo-account.html#ixzz17q9Tp6Tk

In the meantime, here are some pretty straightforward steps that even a dumb pigfuck like you should be able to follow:

1. Log into your primary Yahoo account. Yahoo will link your newly created fake disposable email address to this account.

2. Go to the options/mail options menu located in the upper right of your Yahoo mail page.

3. Look under the Spam section for "AddressGuard" when you land on the Yahoo Mail Options page. Select the Address Guard link.

4. Click either "Create a Disposable Address" or "Get Started Now." (Either may show up, both will take you to where you need to go.)

5. Use the prompts shown to create the name for your disposable fake email address.

6. Set the preferences for your new fake address once your name is created. Preferences include where to direct messages and a color code for your email inbox.

7. Click setup AddressGuard when you're done. You're now ready to use your new disposable email address.

Best,

Lizzy>

<Dear Lizzy,
  Is it working?>
  Best,
  Nemo>

<Like a charm. I'd never be able to figure out who "crazedcop-
  per1" is.>

<great. TYVM>

<YW>

<cunt>

<pigfuck>

A bad month had just gotten a good deal worse for Chief Inspector Svenjamin Bubbles. The headline of the *Aftonbladet* showed a picture of Jessie framed in what looked like a sheriff's poster from the Wild West:

WANTED: DEAD OR ALIVE.
CONTACT: INSPECTOR LIGHTYEAR

The *Svenska Dagbladet* more soberly editorialized:

This most recent fiasco raises anew the question whether the national police force performs any useful function whatsoever. Eliminating the police would, in a time of budgetary constraints and economic contraction, open up valuable funds for additional child-care and preschool centers as well as badly needed subsidies to the domestic organic knit wool sweater industry, which still hasn't fully absorbed the market dislocations caused by the advent of synthetic fleece.

And Oslo's leading daily, the *Aftenposten*, in a clear case of schadenfreude, ran the mocking headline:

SWEDISH POLICE HOLD PIXAR CHARACTER IN MURDER CASE.

The fact that it took the force nearly forty-eight hours to figure out how to remove the video from its own official Web site hadn't contributed to its reputation as an elite outfit.

Bubbles had been reduced to asking Salamander for help. Not that any was forthcoming.

"Now was that really necessary?" Bubbles stood akimbo before the entrance to her cell.

"You're the one who arrested me for murder," Salamander said, all the while performing her commando push-ups.

"That's because you committed murder."

She didn't answer.

"Well, I'd appreciate it if you'd remove the video. Posthaste."

Salamander looked up from her push-ups long enough to flash the inspector her blankest expression. "I have no idea what you're talking about."

"And I thought we were making progress," Bubbles said.

"I guess not."

"So you won't take it down?"

"Not unless you give me back my mainframe."

"I'm not in the business of negotiating with killers."

"Suit yourself. Only I didn't murder anyone. At least not those two losers."

Now after all this headache, Bubbles was eagerly awaiting the pathology report about the severed pinkie from the Digit Division of the Royal Pathological Institute. But when he opened his email, his stomach dropped. His inbox was cluttered with 130,000 messages. Several issued from his newfound fans around the globe.

Swedish police, what a friggin' oxymoron. —Jaagup P., Tallinn, Estonia

Bubbles winced. But he couldn't really expect more from an Estonian.

Inspector, I've discovered a mouse with very large round ears and a squeaky voice who I believe has been selling crystal meth. —Paul G., Paris, France

Most hilarious, indeed. And sooo original. A nation still smarting from its shameful performance in World War II.

文字及び仮名遣の研究(橋本進吉博士著作集　第冊‐岩波書店!!!!!!

Same to you, pal. And many more.

At least a few messages were sincere; Bubbles found himself unexpectedly touched and grateful for the support that trickled in from distant corners:

Dear Inspector, Hard as it may be for you to believe, I know exactly what you're going through. Today's gotcha media are always out for blood. Hang tough, my friend.

Fondly,

Mark Furman (formerly LAPD) Hollywood, CA

The remaining 129,987 messages were of a different character:

Swedish Penis Enlarger!!! Half-price sale, today only. This silicone vacuum pump (patent pending) promises to permanently expand the muscle that matters most. Special discount for Danish men.

DEAR BUBBLES, I AM MOVED TO WRITE YOU THIS LETTER, THIS WAS IN CONFIDENCE CONSIDERING MY PRESENT CIRCUMSTANCE. I ESCAPED ICELAND FINANCIAL COLLAPSE WITH MY WIFE AND CHILDREN, FOUND ASYLUM IN NIGERIA. HOWEVER DUE TO THIS SITUATION I CHANGED MY BILLIONS OF DOLLARS DEPOSITED IN SWISS BANK INTO MONEY CODED FOR SAFE PURPOSE BECAUSE . . .

SUBJECT: Bring back time when beautiful big breasty Latvian girls were yours.

Boost your sexual strength with our meds!

Be Norwegian sexual giant all night long.

Discounts and perfect prices only for you.

We know solution you are looking for!

Imagine if you had the chance to buy a Wal-Mart franchise in Greenland right when it first opened its doors there and all you needed was a small stake to get in? Hurry, to buy NOW. This opportunity will NOT last forever!

Bubbles opened the door to Salamander's cell. "You win. You get the mainframe back."

She glanced up from *Tensor Field Equations*, third edition. "Great. Give me a few minutes and your spam filters will be back in place."

The inspector returned to his computer to find the spam had vanished. Just ten messages now, nine notes of derision and mockery and one from Professor Dr. Crabo Sologrub, head of the Digits Division of the Royal Pathological Institute.

<I have the results of the pinkie autopsy. We should talk.>

The coyote howl ringtone sounded on Blomberg's Motorola i1 Droid with 2.1 Backflip update. He had just walked into Melkkung's Kaffebar, popular with the Järfälla day-trading scene. He needed a caffeine infusion. "Blomberg here."

"Hello, I was trying to reach Mr. Stiggi."

"Hello, Erotikka."

"Oh, Mikael, it's you. I was hoping you could put Stiggi on the line."

"Erotikka, Stiggi's indisposed at the moment."

"Oh, dear, I hope it's nothing serious. Can you leave him a message? Tell him his friends Boo and Baa miss him dearly. They want him to come and play."

"Okay, sweetheart."

"Did you get the message?"

"I think so."

"Repeat it back to me."

"Erotikka, love, I'm at the dentist. I've just been called in for my appointment."

"Why are you at the dentist?"

"To have my teeth cleaned, dear."

"Promise me you're not there to have them whitened. I love your coffee- and nicotine-stained teeth exactly as they are."

"Okay, I promise."

"Men have their teeth whitened only when they're having an affair. You're not having an affair, are you, Mikael?"

"Only with you, love."

"Swear?"

"Yes, I swear."

"Don't forget to give Stiggi the message from Boo and Baa."

"I won't."

"Mikael?"

"Yes?"

"I love you."

"Okay, dear. Me, too."

"Me, too, what?"

"I love you, too."

"Mikael?"

"Yes?"

"Why don't you ever say it first?"

"Say what?"

"You know."

"Sometimes I do. But just not in the dentist's office. You know I love you."

"Okay, bye. And don't forget to give the message to Stiggi."

Blomberg buried his face in his hands. *She's out of control.* Erotikka had once been an accomplished editor at *Millennium*, a force to be reckoned with. But ever since being downsized, she'd turned increasingly promiscuous. Without steady work to focus her considerable energies, she found release only in exhausting erotic marathons that would make any Dane blush. Something had to give. Perhaps she could do some volunteer work in a Nordic folklore or renewable energy organization. In the meantime, he'd just have to hang in there. On his Droid, he made a notation: "Buy groceries. Bring Erotikka to multiple simultaneous orgasms."

Blomberg ordered another trough of Kibbutz-Grown Bitter Peacenik Roast and lit a hand-rolled cigarette.

The waiter brought him his trough. "As of the fifteenth, there's only smoking outdoors. Sorry."

Blomberg glanced outdoors, where several smokers were frozen solid on the sidewalk. He extinguished his cigarette and stashed it in his tobacco pouch for later. As a consolation, he then ordered a side of fried eel. *After all, I am smoking less.*

Then he opened his laptop and made a list of all the things he knew about the girl with the Baltic sturgeon tattoo, underlining *Baltic*.

Height: Between 4'10"and 4'11"
Weight: 90–95 pounds
Dress: Prefers black. T-shirt indicates possible interests in ornithology, automatic weapons, and Saturday morning cartoons.

Skills: Bushido samurai techniques and Kurai Kotori ninja swordmanship.

Brain lateralization: Right-handed, yet takes penalty kicks with left foot.

Markings: Baltic sturgeon (*Acipenser sturio*) tattoo.

Hair: Dyed black. Natural blond.

Blomberg lapped up the last of his Ecuadoran Save-the-Tortoise Roast and wiped his fingers, greasy from the fried eel, on a napkin. All at once it came to him. *Amy Winehouse.* But on Yahoo! ANSWERS he learned that Winehouse had a Betty Boop tattoo where the sturgeon had to be. And was a natural brunette. And was left-handed.

Then he thought back to the family photo on Salamander's UKEA nightstand, the twin sisters flanking their father, the handsome KGB double-agent psychopath.

"Chamelea," he whispered to himself.

As if Salamander had again hacked directly into his cerebral cortex, he heard a mocking voice in response. "Took you long enough, Kalle Fucking Blomberg."

EIGHT

MÅNDAG, FEBRUARI 7–TISDAG, FEBRUARI 8

Decapitation is NOT a victimless crime!
—UPPSALA PROVINCIAL SJUKHUSET HOSPITAL,
DECAPITATION SUPPORT GROUP

Bubbles arrived at the 172-square-foot office of Professor Dr. Crabo Sologrub. The doctor stood six foot two and had blond hair and blue eyes. *How distinctive*, thought Bubbles. They shook hands, and the professor promptly washed his for thirty seconds in a ball of antibacterial foam.

A cleanliness nut, thought Bubbles. *Or an anti-Semite.*

"I believe you've already met with my colleague, Doktor Svenssen," said Professor Dr. Sologrub.

"Yes, Professor Doktor Svenssen gave me a general description of the assailant based on the strangulation marks."

"Sven is very knowledgeable about reindeer," said Professor Dr. Sologrub dismissively. "But technically speaking, he does not have a full academic appointment, and so 'Doktor' is sufficient. And I'm afraid he knows very little about pinkies."

He placed the severed digit on a large metallic table. "As you can see, this pinkie is enormous."

"Doktor Svenssen estimated that it belonged to a man seven feet tall."

Professor Dr. Sologrub shook his head. "This is what I mean when you let a reindeer specialist stray into pinkie matters. Your assailant is exactly seven foot three."

"Svenssen put his weight at 300 pounds."

"My analysis of the lipid content and congealed fatty acid content suggests a weight of 277 pounds."

"So my assailant is taller and leaner than Svenssen suggested."

"Precisely."

"Possibly a onetime basketball player?"

"It's a possibility. Though the metacarpal tissue shows none of the chronic swelling or enlargement typical of professional basketball players. Occasional play in a intramural league can't be excluded."

Bubbles scribbled away in his notebook. He preferred pen and paper, though he did own a BlackBerry 9800 Torch, which he used only for calls and texting.

Professor Sologrub deftly turned the pinkie with a forceps. "As you can see, the nail shows signs of a recent manicure."

A gigantic psychopathic reindeer strangler with a touch of vanity, thought Bubbles.

"Several strands of lower knuckle hair clearly indicate that your killer is a natural blond, if I may put it like that."

"Would you describe the amount of knuckle hair as excessive?"

"What do you mean?"

"I mean, do you think we're looking for an unusually hirsute blond seven foot three 277-pound psychopath?"

"No, I would describe the hair growth as quite average. But

there is another feature of our giant that *is* most extraordinary. Look carefully at the severing."

The professor held up the pinkie for Bubbles's inspection. It was not a pretty sight. Bubbles forced himself to look closely.

"Yes?"

"Note that the wound is not clean. Or let me be more precise. The wound indicates that the pinkie was not sliced off in one fell swoop."

"I'm not sure I follow."

"In most cases of pinkie severance, the accident occurs all at once. The butcher misses with his boning knife and off comes the pinkie. But in this case, the pinkie was severed only after repeated cuts."

"Are you telling me that someone else cut off the killer's pinkie?"

"That was my original surmise. Until I did a DNA analysis. I discovered something rather remarkable."

'Rather'! What is with these scientists at the Royal Institute?

"You see, it appears that your giant feels no pain."

"I would think that's quite common among serial killers," said Bubbles.

"You don't understand me, Inspector. I mean, this killer is physiologically *incapable* of feeling pain. It's a rare genetic disorder called congenital analgesia, or CIPA."

"You're saying this giant kept hacking away, not realizing that he was also cutting his finger, until finally it fell off?"

"Precisely."

All at once Bubbles turned deathly pale. Sologrub thought the odor of formaldehyde and the sight of the grisly digit had finally gotten to the inspector. So he was baffled when he heard Bubbles whisper under his breath, "Niemand, Ronni Niemand. How could I be so dense?"

Blomberg sipped a bowl of Sierra Madre Dignity-to-Donkeys Quadruple Roast at Elevira's, a new kaffeklub in Modershalm popular with the jet-setting crowd of Malmafjärding litigators.

"What can I get you?" asked Blomberg.

"I'll just have an herbal tea," said his companion, Sveet Flogbard.

Herbal tea, thought Blomberg. *He really is pretty far gone.*

A starting center for the talented Swedish national soccer teams of the late 1980s, Flogbard had once been considered the most creative midfielder of his generation. But then a misplayed ball in a World Cup qualifying match against Denmark had effectively ended his career. He became a national pariah, hounded by hate mail and death threats. He sought refuge in Absolut and northern Lapland, where for the last two decades he'd worked anonymously for the Swedish Royal Census Bureau. At the time of the millennial census in 2000, he'd met Blomberg, who'd been writing an exposé about extortion, incest, and crimes against humanity at the Swedish Registry of Parishes. The two had become friendly and Flogbard had remained a valuable contact ever since.

"Were you able to learn anything about Chamelea Salamander?" asked Blomberg.

"A bit. According to hospital records, she was born five minutes after her fraternal twin sister, the one who's often in the news."

Blomberg noticed that Flogbard's hand visibly trembled as he lifted the herbal tea. *It really was a very easy ball to clear. And it did result in our elimination from the World Cup, and worse yet, Denmark's qualification. Still, the man has suffered enough.*

"School records confirm that Chamelea was always the superior pupil. In kindergarten she excelled in finger painting and gingersnap design. By contrast, her sister was disciplined for biting her teacher in the larynx after the latter compared her to Pippi Longstocking."

A sensitivity of long standing.

"Chamelea continued to excel all through elementary school, particularly in figure skating and knitting. At her sixth-grade graduation ceremony, she won the coveted Most Likely to Conform and Most Likely to Pay Taxes Without Cheating awards. Her sister, by contrast, continued to get into trouble. She failed all her classes except math and was suspended for blowing up the boys' hockey team."

Already good at math.

"What did you expect?" Salamander hacked into his brain.

"After her father was set aflame, everything changed for Chamelea. She was sent to Germany to live with relatives."

Relatives? What relatives?

"She stayed in Germany for a number of years. Where isn't exactly clear. She appears to have finished a degree in graphic design. It seems, though, that she struggled with the disintegration of her family and the immolation of her father. Apparently she'd been quite close to Kalashnikov. Now he refused to see her, presumably because he didn't want her to see him in his horribly disfigured state. So she drifted into sexual promiscuity, having numerous casual, vaguely self-destructive affairs with third-rate German conceptual artists."

These census takers in Lapland know a lot.

"She returned to Sweden shortly after her twenty-first birthday. After six months of casual sex and recreational drug use, she settled down, taking a job doing industrial design for UKEA."

"Did you say UKEA?"

"Yes. It's the world largest producer of self-assembly fake teak bookcases."

"Of course. How long did Chamelea work there?"

"For around three years. Then she suddenly left. It appears she returned to Germany. In any case, that's where her trail goes dead."

That is, until she appears on a surveillance camera decapitating an unpublished thriller writer.

Chief Inspector Bubbles arrived at police headquarters at the crack of dawn. Which, this being February, was at 10:20 AM. He wasted no time with small talk. He knew he was on the cusp of an important discovery. "Officer Flunk, bring me the file on Ronni Niemand."

"Yes, Chief Inspector."

Two hours passed and still Bubbles had received nothing. He called Flunk back to his office. "The file."

"Excuse me, Chief. It was my morning to drive our daughter for her allergy shots. Now I have an appointment with my therapist." Flunk was still prone to crying jags after the discovery of the murdered reindeer family. The force paid for lifelong massage and psychoanalysis for police officers who had suffered trauma in or near the line of duty. "Can I get you the file after my therapy appointment?"

"When will that be?"

"In three hours."

"Can't you get the file in the meantime?"

"I fear it will stir up depressing associations."

"I understand. After your session, then."

As soon as Flunk left his office, Inspector Bubbles summoned Officer Snorkkle. "Bring me the Niemand file."

"What do you say?"

Bubbles glared at this subordinate. "*Please.*"

"Yes, sir."

Snorkkle reported back two hours later. "We can't find the file, sir."

"How can that be?" Even if Salamander had erased it, a hard copy was always kept in police archives.

"I don't know, sir."

"Well, keep looking . . . *please.*"

"Yes, sir."

Another hour passed. There was no sign of Snorkkle, but Flunk appeared in the doorway of the chief's office. "May I?"

"Of course, come in Flunk."

"May I close the door, sir?"

"Certainly."

Flunk shut the door and stood before the chief's desk nervously fingering his blue and yellow police-issue knit ski hat.

"So, how was your session, Flunk?"

"I thought we worked through some important material involving my childhood fear of the Moomins."

"I'm glad to hear that."

"Chief?"

"Yes, Flunk?"

"Is it true that you asked Officer Snorkkle to bring you the Niemand file?"

"Why, yes."

Flunk's lower lip trembled. "Sir, you specifically asked *me* to bring you that file."

"Flunk, you were at therapy."

"Sir, you specifically said that you could wait until I returned."

"I'm sorry, Officer. Time was of the essence."

"Then why did you say you could wait?"

"I don't recall what I said."

"I feel I must file a workplace grievance, sir."

Bubbles drew a deep breath. *Things must be better in Greenland.* "Now why would you want to do that, Officer?"

"Sir, I feel that you're punishing me for seeking therapeutic help for a psychic injury I suffered in or near the line of duty."

"How on earth am I punishing you?"

"Please, don't raise your voice, sir. That's also actionable."

"I apologize, Officer. How am I punishing you?"

"By reassigning my work, sir. By making me feel marginal and without value to the force because I've sought help for a work-related psychic wound."

"That certainly wasn't my intention, Flunk."

"Intention isn't relevant according to the statute, sir. What's relevant is my perception of your behavior."

From the back pocket of his police-issue corduroy Nordic knickers, Flunk removed a copy of the Public Law 2.102 §4(a):

The workplace is to be a place of maximum dignity and re-spect for all. Jokes are permitted, as long as laughter does not offend any Person (real or imagined), Group, or Other Life-

Form. The employer is responsible for maintaining a workplace conducive to the health, welfare, and erotic satisfaction of his or her employees. Any failure to do so is actionable under PL 4.42 §6(c).

"I'm sorry, Officer. My bad entirely." Bubbles punched his chest in frank acknowledgment of his transgression. "The fact is that Officer Snorkkle was unable to locate the Niemand file. So I would be grateful if you'd coordinate the search."

"Really, sir?"

"Really, Officer."

"I'd be delighted, sir." The chief and the officer exchanged an awkward hug.

An hour later Flunk returned to the chief's office. "Still searching, sir."

"Thank you for the update, Flunk."

Shortly before lunch the next day, Officer Flunk entered Bubbles's office, beaming. "The file, sir."

"Excellent, Flunk. Good work."

Minutes later, Officer Snorkkle poked his head in the chief's office. "You know why the moron was able to find the file? Because *he* was the one who'd misfiled it in the first place. He'd put it under R for Ronni. Fucking retarded Finn."

"Watch your mouth, Officer."

Bubbles drained his flask of Pepto-Bismol and swallowed four ibuprofen. His parents had wanted him to become a doctor. They were appalled by his decision to enter the force. *A schande,* lamented his father. *And he was always so good at math, a real wizard,* his mother would say. Maybe it wasn't too late to enter the family pharmaceutical business.

The Niemand file confirmed what Bubbles remembered about the case. Nearly three years ago, Niemand had killed and mutilated two police officers with his bare hands. A national manhunt ensued. It ended not with Niemand's apprehension, but with the discovery of his body in a deserted factory building. He'd been stapled to the ceiling with an industrial nail gun. His eyes had been gouged out, his arms hacked off, and all his internal organs removed. His tongue had been cut off and inserted in his anus, while his testicles had been stuffed in his mouth. Police had rushed Niemand to a local hospital, but efforts at resuscitation had failed. The killer or killers had never been found; the police surmised that robbery had not been the motive.

But Bubbles wasn't concerned about solving the cold case. His concern was the Reindeer Ripper, and now he was forced to consider the unhappy possibility that Niemand had either risen from the dead or been cloned. He dismissed the former out of hand and decided that the latter was also unlikely.

Flipping to the back of the Niemand file, Bubbles was surprised to come across classified documents marked "Cosmic Top Secret." Only recently added to the dossier, these documents had been transferred to the police directly from Säpo, the Swedish secret police. A memo from the director of the agency, itself marked *Restricted,* indicated Säpo's willingness to share its most sensitive file with the police, now that the material had already been posted for several months on Wikileaks.

Wikileaks, Bubbles wrote in his notebook. *Must check this out.*

The information confirmed that Niemand was the son of Dmitri Kalashnikov, the worthless KGB agent whose defection to Sweden had led to the creation of a multibillion-kronor ultrasecret autocratic genocidal shadow regime in the heart of the Swedish government whose sole purpose was to hide the former agent's acts of spousal abuse. According to the Säpo file, Niemand's mother had been an East German Stasi agent/Olympic swimmer with whom Kalashnikov had had an affair during an assignment in Berlin. After the wall came down, the mother had had a sex change operation, but it was unclear to which gender. Now he or she ran a haircutting boutique in the Prenzlauer Berg section of Berlin.

Bubbles continued to read the file. Niemand had been raised in Leipzig, East Germany, where he'd excelled in Greco-Roman wrestling, perhaps on account of his genetic immunity to pain. According to one newspaper account, he'd won a regional competition even after suffering a compound fracture of his right forearm in an early round that left him wrestling with exposed bone. It was speculated that the East Germans, eager to promote such a talent to the international level, had placed Niemand on a regimen of equine growth hormone, which might have contributed to his unusual size. In any case, Niemand never fulfilled the hopes of the GDR's Greco-Roman Wrestling and Human Guinea Pig Federation. His genetic mutation proved more of a handicap than an advantage, as his multiple fractures would often get infected and take months to heal. He did, however, manage to take "show" in the Dresden Derby, East Germany's premier race for Thoroughbreds. He then worked briefly as a wrestling coach, but was dismissed after strangling several pupils. After the collapse of the Soviet empire, he moved to Sweden and worked for his father, helping in various projects of rape and assassination. The file assessed his intelligence as below average, his command of languages other than German as poor, and his affect as withdrawn:

For a brutal psychopathic giant, Niemand is prone to self-pity, petulance, and multiple phobias. A confirmed bed wetter, he is afraid of the dark and always sleeps with a Santa night-light. He has never married, has no meaningful relationships, and generally eschews contact with others, as he considers all human beings deserving of violent death—the exception being his deep, profound, and frankly tender bond with his identical twin brother, Reinhard.

Bubbles sat bolt upright in his office chair and shouted into his office intercom: "Flunk, contact our friends in the Verfassungsschutz Polizei and the Bundesnachrichtendienst in Germany. Ask them for whatever info they have on Reinhard Niemand . . . *please.*"

"When you hired me, you neglected to tell me that Twig had been convicted of negligent destruction of a method of birth control and of having semi-consensual intercourse with a drowsy woman."

Blomberg sat with Twig's father, Nix Arssen, in Sonja's, a new kaffebar in Slöttersol popular with Pontonjärbataljonen's young commodity brokers. They both were lapping Peruvian High Octaine Sherpa's Blend from ceramic paint buckets.

Arssen looked down and spoke softly. "Yes, I owe you an apology. I'm ashamed of my absence of candor. But I feared that you would not accept the assignment if I told you."

Blomberg nodded. "You also neglected to mention that your father was institutionalized at UKEA for most of his professional life."

"That was a sincere omission. You must believe me."

Blomberg studied Arssen closely. He appeared to be telling the truth. "In any case, I thought I should bring you up to speed on my findings. I assume you've been following the developments in the media."

"I know that that police have arrested Jessie the cowgirl for the murder of my son."

"You watched the video?"

"It was hard to avoid. It was difficult to watch my son's head being kicked like a soccer ball by a Pixar figure."

"I'm very sorry you had to endure that. You know, of course, that the police's real suspect is Lizzy Salamander."

"The scrawny psychopathic hackstar. I understand she was also responsible for the video. I fear the police are completely un-equipped to deal with her."

"Only I'm positive that Lizzy had nothing to do with Twig's murder. In fact, I believe she was framed. The murder was care-fully choreographed to make it look like the work of Salamander. Evidently the real murderer is Salamander's fraternal twin, Cha-melea."

"Chamelea? I never knew Salamander had a twin."

"Few people did. Only those who followed Lizzy's life story carefully."

"Why would the twin want to kill my son and frame her sister?"

"Relations between the two sisters were never good. Salaman-der tried to run her twin over with a tricycle that Chamelea got for her third birthday. Evidently Salamander had wanted a tricycle, too, but instead she got a rock. Two years later, she tossed Chame-lea from a tree house. Things got worse after Chamelea witnessed Salamander roasting marshmallows on their burning father. So

Chamelea may have been eager for revenge. As for Chamelea's motive for killing Twig, that's where things get murky. But I have a theory. You see, Chamelea used to work for UKEA."

"When was this?"

"From 2004 until 2007. I have a hunch that Dagher Ukea hired Chamelea to kill Twig. He framed Salamander to make the murder look like a vigilante gender killing. But his real interest was in the manuscript. A book documenting Hitler's role in designing the popular Svengig coffee table could ruin the company. I believe he wanted to get his hands on the manuscript before anyone else could, simply in order to destroy it. In this latter regard, I fear he has succeeded all too brilliantly. The undoctored video from the crime scene shows Chamelea leaving with what appears to be Twig's laptop in her backpack."

Arssen shook his head. "The killer may have made off with Twig's laptop, but not with his manuscript."

"How can you be certain?"

"Because Twig typed all his books on a typewriter. My son was something of a romantic. He once read that Peter Høeg typed *Smilla's Sense of Snow* on a manual Hermes Portable. Ever since then he followed Høeg's example."

"I never understood the enthusiasm over *Smilla*; I found the book entirely mediocre."

"As did I. It indulged every stereotype of Greenland. But Twig was superstitious. He bought a Hermes Portable on eBay, hoping to match Høeg's success. And while Høeg became an international publishing phenomenon, my son managed only to be an unpublished victim of decapitation." Arssen bitterly sipped the dregs from his bucket of coffee. "In any case, Twig used his computer only to blog, not that anyone ever read his posts."

"At least we know that Ukea doesn't have Twig's manuscript. Which means, he—or at least his hireling Chamelea—is still actively searching for it. Do you think it's possible that Chamelea ever met your father?"

"Impossible. My father entered UKEA's psychiatric ward in the early 1970s, never to emerge."

"When did he die?"

"My father is still alive."

"What? Why, he must be nearly . . ."

"He turns one hundred next August."

"And for the last forty years he's been institutionalized."

"More like fifty."

"Can I interview him?"

"I'm afraid it would be pointless. He's quite far gone. Dementia."

"I see." Bubbles stared into the oily surface of his coffee. He was sorely tempted to order a plate of fried eels. "Only one thing continues to baffle me, the murder of Jerker Ekkrot."

"The author of *The Life Cycle of the Baltic Sturgeon, with Particular Attention to Matters of Coastline Breeding*?"

"One and the same. I assume that Chamelea also murdered Ekkrot. But I have no idea why. There are some intriguing connections. Chamelea has a Baltic sturgeon tattoo across her back and neck."

"Are you sure it's not a Siberian sturgeon?"

"Quite positive. But a connection between her tattoo and Ekkrot's work? That I don't know. I also learned from a source close to the investigation—I have to protect his identity, but let's just say he's the chief investigator on the case—that Twig and Ekkrot exchanged several cell phone conversations in the weeks before they were murdered. Do you know anything about this?"

"Twig and Jerker Ekkrot had been inseparable friends for decades."

"I thought you said that Twig had no friends at all."

"This was the one exception."

"Your son and his best friend are murdered within days of each other, and you neglect to mention this connection?"

"Again, an honest omission."

"In any case. What can you tell me about Twig and Ekkrot?"

"It's a rather long story. Twig was a singularly untalented child. Like a typical Swedish father, I bought him his first pair of soccer cleats when he was still in the crib, but he showed no interest in the game, not even in corner kicks and set pieces. He likewise showed no interest in traditional Nordic sports. He took his first and last ninety-meter ski jump when he was five. The results were . . . not good.

"Twig remained a difficult boy, always contrary. 'I wish I were Dutch,' he would cry. Needless to say this wounded me deeply. He read widely, but only Norwegians. He loved Knut Hamsun, above all. Imagine! That madman from Oslo! Later it was Ibsen. I brought him to psychiatrists, but nothing helped. At school he was bullied and ostracized. Twice he failed the state exam in standardized thinking and rote memorization.

"This was the time of Björn Borg's great triumphs, so I hoped that tennis might interest Twig. After all, it was a sport more associated with America and Australia than our homeland. So I built a court in our yard on a frozen lake and enrolled Twig in the Royal Tennis Academy. But this too turned into a disaster. Needless to say, all the pupils were taught the two-handed backhand in the style of Borg, but Twig rebelled. He wanted to hit a one-hander, like John McEnroe. I tried to reason with him, but it was hopeless. The Academy produced many top players—Edberg, of course, and Wilander, too, whose struggles with Nordic Dullness Syndrome you have so sensitively described."

"Thank you."

"But Twig never even managed to learn to hit a reliable forehand. His serve lacked punch, he was timid at the net, and his footwork was clumsy. In short, the ten years of lessons were a total waste. There was only one other pupil at the academy nearly as weak as Twig."

"Jerker Ekkrot."

"Exactly. Ekkrot was also hopeless. Although he accepted the two-handed backhand, he had something against topspin. As a consequence, he hit a flat forehand—and predictably, his ball always sailed deep. Like Twig, he was sullen and withdrawn. In breaks between overhead and volley drills, he'd lock himself in the bathroom and read Kierkegaard. He liked nothing better than to idle by the baseline, racket at this side, mocking the Nobel Committee for Literature. 'Just look at the list of laureates. D. H. Lawrence—no! Kafka—no! Joyce—no! Proust—no! Nabokov—no! Borges—no! Who gets it? *Pearl S. Buck. Sinclair Lewis.* What a joke!'

"So Twig and Ekkrot became fast friends. Together they tried their hand at writing science fiction—vile, anti-Swedish science fiction that always involved the thermonuclear destruction of Stockholm by Norwegian-speaking aliens. Of course Ekkrot later matured. He applied himself to his studies and became a prominent scientist, one of the leading sturgeon specialists of his generation. Twig never found his niche. As you know, he was an indifferent student in journalism school. In contrast to some of his fellow students, he never went on to write prizewinning exposés of obstruction of justice, organ harvesting, and buggery in the Swedish Cross-Country Skiing Federation."

Blomberg accepted the compliment with a nod.

"And of course nothing came of his dreams of literary glory." Arssen released a deep, melancholy sigh.

"Do you have any idea what Twig and Ekkrot might have spoken about in the days before they were murdered?"

"I'm afraid not," said Arssen bitterly. "For that you'll need to ask Fröken Chamelea Salamander."

"Or Dagher Ukea," hacked Salamander into Blomberg's brain.

NINE

$$ds^2 = -\left(1 - \frac{2KM}{c^2 r}\right) c^2\, dt^2 + \left(\frac{1}{1 - \dfrac{2KM}{c^2 r}}\right) dr^2 + r^2\, (d\theta^2 + \sin^2\theta\, d\varphi^2)$$

Officer Flunk tapped on the door to Chief Inspector Bubbles's office. "Sir, we've just received the Niemand file from our friends in the Gestapo."

Bubbles cleared his voice. "That's not what the German secret police are called these days, Flunk."

The officer silently placed the file on the chief inspector's desk and began to tiptoe away.

"Flunk?"

"Yes, sir?"

"When you contacted our German colleagues, did you use that term?"

"Sir, I was just following the form printed in *How to Address Queries, Inquiries, and Requests to Other European Police Departments.*"

"Bring me the book immediately."

Flunk returned with the yellowed and heavily dog-eared volume.

Bubbles flipped through some samples. "My Dear SS Hauptsturm-bannführer."

He examined the copyright—1941.

"This volume is badly out-of-date. Where's the more recent edition?"

Flunk shrugged.

Bubbles felt his blood pressure rise to 172 over 120. From the top drawer of his desk, he removed his political fallout timer. In two hours the call would come from the prime minister's office. An hour later, the article in the *Aftonbladet*. Thirty minutes after that, the official protest from the German government and the incensed words from the German ambassador. Then the evening press conference with Bubbles's abject apology. The editorials in the morning papers calling for his resignation. Then the 10:00 AM official kiss and make up between the German ambassador and the Swedish foreign minister. Twenty-four hours of hell.

I'll probably drop dead of a heart attack before I ever get that bungalow in Greenland.

Door to his office closed, flask of Pepto-Bismol open on his desk, Bubbles examined the file from the Bundesnachrichten-dienst. It confirmed that Reinhard Niemand was Ronni's identical twin. Like Ronni, Reinhard suffered from congenital analgesia and had also tried his hand at Greco-Roman wrestling, but without his brother's success. In trade school, he had studied to become a chef, but was forced to give this up as a result of a pattern of inadvertently lighting himself on fire. Next he studied to become a master cabinetmaker, but after a brief apprenticeship with a branch of UKEA in Hamburg, he was let go, again apparently as a result of a tendency to accidentally saw through his own bones and organs. He'd done some minor work for his father—

helping him repair a lakeside cottage and dispose of the bodies of several Russian prostitutes—but otherwise had kept a low profile. The Germans were unable to account for his whereabouts over the last two years.

Bubbles took a swig of the antacid and mentally inventoried the case. He didn't like the conclusion staring him in the face. Until this moment, he had worked from the assumption that on his plate were two distinct cases. One involved the murder by decapitation of two writers: the first, a noted authority on the Baltic Sturgeon; the second, an unpublished writer of bad thrillers. Yet both writers had histories of insensitivity toward women. The assailant, a self-styled gender vigilante, was in custody. Case seemingly closed.

The second involved a Reindeer Ripper. Although disturbing, this case also seemed straightforward. Serial reindeer killers like to kill reindeer. It's as simple as that. He remembered a lecture he'd once attended at the Royal Forensic Institute on Psychological Profiling of the Serial Reindeer Killer. The lecturer, one of the most highly respected experts on reindeer-related violence in all of Scandinavia, concluded that most killers fell into one of three groups: those who'd had a bad experience with a reindeer in their infancy, those who were working out some misplaced Santa rage, and those with a perverse lust for antlers. But Bubbles vividly remembered the lecturer's conclusion. "Reindeer ripping is a crime of compulsion, not of logic. We are dealing with persons who kill not for advantage or gain but because they must do so. They live to kill reindeer."

Now that he had a suspect, Bubbles began to have his doubts. Ronni Niemand had been a vicious methodical hit man, not a serial killer. To the contrary. He had killed remorselessly and brutally and frequently, but always purposively. If Reinhard was anything like his deceased identical twin, then he was also probably more a seven-foot genetically defective sociopath than a serial reindeer killer. And the facts just didn't make sense. Reinhard was German. *There are no reindeer in Germany.* He just didn't fit the profile of a reindeer ripper.

But most troubling was the connection to Lizzy Salamander. Salamander and Niemand were both the children of Dmitri Kalashnikov. Applying the transitive property, this meant that Niemand was Salamander's half brother. While coincidence couldn't be ruled out, Bubbles's instincts told him otherwise. So for the first time, the chief inspector faced the unwelcome fact that the two sets of killings, which all along he assumed were unrelated, were in fact connected. And if the killings *were* related, then some very big piece of the puzzle was missing. In fact, it would be fair to say *the puzzle itself was missing.* All he had was a bunch of pieces. Which he'd have to look at more carefully. Starting with the surveillance tape of Arssen's decapitation.

"Ah, Mister Blomquvist, please come in." Dagher Ukea extended his long, aristocratic, immaculately manicured hand in greeting.

"Blomberg."

"Ah, yes, I'd forgotten your recent ethnic discovery." Ukea smiled coldly, revealing his uncommonly white teeth and his razor-sharp incisors. His office appeared somewhat larger than Blomberg remembered—now closer to 400 square feet. *Maybe the ceiling's been raised.* On the wall were framed photos of UKEA folding chairs.

"In any case," Ukea continued, "it is a surprise seeing you again."

"And why is that?"

Ukea laughed. "I might have thought that by now you would have met with a fatal accident."

A strangely aggressive response.

Ukea stared at Blomberg icily through his polar ice blue eye. His other eye was covered in an eye patch, also something new.

"It looks like you're the one who's had an accident," Blomberg observed.

"A small mishap during a recent ice-fishing trip."

"Fishing for Baltic sturgeon?"

Ukea's one good eye narrowed. "As you know, Mr. Blomberg, the Baltic sturgeon is an endangered fish. We were more interested in catching the jewfish."

"Now called the goliath grouper."

"I confess, I'm not up on the most recent politically correct fish nomenclature."

"And grouper aren't found in the Baltic or North Sea."

"Ah, perhaps explaining why we caught so few." Ukea suddenly snapped forward in his UKEA Master of the Universe leather chair. "Come, Mr. Blomberg. I'm a very busy man. Today I must review our entire new fall line of modular sofas. You have fifteen minutes."

Modular sofas originally designed by Adolf Hitler?

Blomberg kept the question to himself. It was pointless to be confrontational. It just made Ukea less cooperative. Just then the door to the spacious office flew open and in trotted two giant mastiffs. They assumed positions flanking Ukea's desk, snarling at Blomberg.

"I hope you don't mind my puppies, Infart and Utfart."

"Not at all. And speaking of modular sofas, I'm looking to get a new one for my living room. I still love my old UKEA couch, but it's getting a bit old. It was from your Bergman line, the Seventh Seal Sofa. You know, Death and the Knight on a chessboard pattern that hardly showed the dirt."

Ukea brightened."I remember it well. After our Strindberg collection, our Bergman line was our most successful. Sadly, the young people of today are less interested in the classics. Now we must appeal to the Boo and Baa generation."

The mention of Boo and Baa made Blomberg blush crimson.

"I take it, Mr. Blomberg, that you've come today to discuss matters other than modular sofas."

"True. As you recall, I'm doing some research for the Arssen family."

"I was under the impression that the police had solved that case."

"Actually, I'm not sure they have." Blomberg shifted forward in his chair. "Do you happen to remember an employee by the name of Chamelea Salamander?"

He watched closely to see how Ukea would respond to the mention of Chamelea. But the CEO didn't bat an eye.

"Yes, of course. Salamander worked as a graphic designer in UKEA's branch in Hultsfred, Småland, from 2004 to 2007, as I recall. She did nice work on our popular Finnbad shower curtain."

Blomberg didn't try to mask his surprise. "Dr. Ukea, UKEA must employ more than 125,000 persons in countries around the world. I find it rather remarkable that you would have such precise memories of an entry-level graphic designer."

Ukea laughed without obvious malice. "Mr. Blomberg. You spoke of 125,000 employees. In fact the precise number is 127,312. This morning we sadly had to fire a shipping clerk in Sri Lanka who stole some bathroom lighting, but happily this loss was more than offset by the hiring of five new employees in our Harmony in the Bedroom line manufactured in Malaysia. It is my business to know as much about our every employee as possible. This was the founding credo of my father, Sløber Ukea. He strongly believed in a new form of capitalism."

From the top drawer of his desk, Ukea removed a pin and handed it to Blomberg.

UKEA: Global Capitalism with a ☺

"May I keep this?"

"By all means. Here, take a few more."

"Tell me more about Sløber."

"My father was a great man, a true visionary. He believed in what he called the third way. When he founded UKEA, Sweden was split between two rival groups. On one side were the fervidly nationalist capitalists, who wanted Sweden to become a global superpower, like the United States. On the other were the communists, who wanted to get rid of the Swedish state altogether and turn all Europe into one giant workers' collective. My father believed it was possible to wed the two competing philosophies. His dream was to unite the socialist's drive to level socioeconomic differences with the nationalist's xenophobic love of fatherland."

"Isn't that called Nazism?"

"Perhaps," said Ukea. "But Sløber always argued that we shouldn't throw out the good of National Socialism with the bad. He used to say, 'Why destroy Albert Speer's beautiful Berlin streetlights just because they lit the path to genocide?'"

Blomberg didn't hazard an answer.

"So I have tried to remain true to my father's founding vision while altering it to accept twenty-first-century realities. I believe Sløber's dream of turning Sweden into a global superpower is no longer attainable. Not with the competition we face from Iceland's geothermal energy and Norway's North Sea oil. But we still remain committed to a form of capitalism that doesn't downsize its workforce at the slightest economic dip, but instead remains loyal to the collective. That is why here at UKEA we encourage our employees to ski together, play tennis together, shop at UKEA together, and to live within five hundred meters of a UKEA store."

"Encourage or require?"

"We believe they are one and the same. That, too, is an article of the UKEA philosophy. And that is why here in Sweden we promise to provide full health-care and educational benefits for all our employees."

"But those benefits are already paid entirely by the state."

"True."

"And in other countries?"

"Sadly we cannot shoulder such exorbitant costs. And of course we must deal with some delicate political situations in our less than stable client states. But in every country that UKEA operates, we guarantee our workers, regardless of age or gender or ethnicity, the most competitive slave wages. Also we also give free T-shirts to our employees at the holidays."

From his desk, Ukea removed a T-shirt from the past Christmas.

UKEA: Global Capitalism with a ☺

"May I keep this, too?"

"I'm afraid this is my last one . . ."

Looks part polyester.

"And our commitment goes beyond holiday T-shirts. We have a long-standing practice of giving all our employees an attractive reindeer-motif cushion for every ten years of service.

Our decade-of-service pillow remains a coveted item, a sign of steady dedication to the corporate collective. Would you like to see one?"

"Please."

Ukea removed a pillow from his desk. *Lots of secret drawers, that desk.* The overstuffed cushion depicted a reindeer grazing by a tree. Blomberg had to admit that in contrast to the T-shirt, the decade-of-service pillow was quite attractive. It would make a nice addition to his shågshäck on Lake Fikmisst. Suddenly he had an image of the pillow wedged under Erotikka's shapely naked buttocks. *Harder, Stiggi, impale me on that muscular Viking shaft!* Blomberg blinked.

"So you see, Mr. Blomberg, this is all of a piece with our corporate ethos. That is why we also maintain state-of-the-art health-care facilities directly on our premises."

"The UKEA Asylum for Workplace Injuries and Criminally Insane Employees?"

"Exactly."

"This is the facility where Twig Arssen's grandfather remains to this day institutionalized?"

"I believe so. And it saddens me to say that Fröken Salamander also has some familiarity with our clinic. It is another, less happy reason why I remember her time at UKEA with extraordinary clarity."

"Chamelea Salamander was also institutionalized?"

"I believe she was kept in our asylum for a year or so."

"Why?"

"Here my memory genuinely fails me."

So much for the extraordinary clarity.

"So Chamelea Salamander isn't presently in your employ?"

Ukea's eye widened in genuine surprise. "In my employ? Mr. Blomberg, I can say without any hesitation that the mere idea is completely preposterous." He laughed explosively to underscore this. The mastiffs howled in unison. "In fact, I think it's fair to say that if Chamelea Salamander suddenly appeared in my office I would have to fear for my life."

"But why?"

"Mr. Blomberg, the fall collection of modular sofas beckons. I've been frank with you. I suggest you direct any further questions to our corporate archives. I believe you're familiar with the facility. And please don't forget your pins."

Chief Inspector Bubbles reviewed the surveillance tape of Arssen's decapitation for the twentieth time. Then he gathered his travel chess set and his MENSA book of puzzles and headed to Salamander's detention cell.

He found her sitting cross-legged on the floor with Officer Snorkkle.

"What's going on?"

"Cunt here is showing me how to download apps onto my iPhone. My wife got me an iPhone for Christmas, our equivalent of Hanukkah—"

"I'm familiar with Christmas, Officer."

"But I've never really used it for anything besides calls and texting. Now it's totally loaded. Check out this app."

Snorkkle showed the chief inspector an application that turned the iPhone into a GPS navigation system with turn-by-turn directions.

"Yes, I've seen this kind of thing before," said Bubbles.

"Okay, then check out IncrediBooth. See, you can use the front-facing camera to create old photo-booth type pictures. Come on, let's give it a go."

The three crowded together for a photo.

"Hey, dumbass," said Salamander, "you got the iPhone facing the wrong direction."

"Whoops, okay. Say *omelett*."

Bubbles inspected the picture. Snorkkle was grinning broadly, Bubbles had instinctively smiled, and Salamander was scowling. *The screen's resolution is far superior to my BlackBerry's.*

"Should we do another?"

"Perhaps later."

"This one's my favorite, Chief. It's called I Love Katamari— totally sick stuff. See, you're the little alien dwarf prince. You push the katamari ball with its adhesive strip through the universe, picking up as much stuff as possible. Just tilt the phone, yeah, like that. And don't skip the dog. You can pick up everything with your katamari. You should see Cunt race through the game. Her top score is like a billion."

"Over," corrected Salamander.

"I haven't even broken a million," said Snorkkle. "But I'm improving." Salamander confirmed this with a nod. "Then we let Flunk try. The moron couldn't even figure out how to pick up the garbage."

Bubbles was surprised to see Salamander and Snorkkle briefly laughing in concert.

"How much to do these apps cost?"

Snorkkle looked down. "Uh . . . the prisoner figured out a way to download them without payment."

Bubbles glared at Snorkkle.

"They're just demos, sir. I swear I'll pay in full once I decide to keep them on my iPhone."

"Okay, Officer. Now if you don't mind, I'd like to speak to Fröken Salamander alone."

"Of course, sir."

Snorkkle and the detainee exchanged good-byes.

"Later, Cunt."

"Pigfuck."

Bubbles took a seat on the floor, awkwardly crossing his legs. "I hope you don't mind if I join you."

"You're the copper. You can do whatever you want."

"I'm glad to see you're getting along better with Officer Snorkkle."

"Pigfuck's okay. He's stopped threatening to anally rape me."

"I'm sure it was all in jest."

Salamander shrugged.

"I've brought the chess set."

Salamander's eyes widened. All games and math quizzes had abruptly stopped with the posting of the cowgirl video on the official police Web site and on YouTube. Nor had they resumed once the video had been taken down.

"Would you like a game?" asked Blomberg.

"Okay."

As usual, Salamander played black. The game opened monotonously, but took an interesting turn when Salamander opted for the Nimzo-Indian Defense.

Interesting. Why didn't she go for the Benko Gambit?

To Bubbles's dismay, Salamander began eating Twinkies between moves. She appeared to swallow them whole.

"That's rather distracting."

Salamander didn't answer. Her mouth was full.

"Do you eat anything besides Twinkies?"

"Pizza."

She gestured to a pile of Big Bill's delivery boxes stacked in the corner of her cell.

"Hardly a healthy diet."

"I have a fast metabolism. And get plenty of exercise." She rolled up a sleeve of her black T-shirt and flexed a bicep menacingly. In front of the 50-inch Bang & Olufsen flat-screen TV that she'd ordered for her cell stood a Precor EFX 5.37 Elliptical Trainer.

"Exercise helps only to a point. When was the last time you had your blood sugar level and triglycerides tested?"

"Whatever."

"Not whatever, Fröken Salamander. You're about to turn thirty. You can't keep abusing your body like you're still some kid in a straitjacket."

Salamander scowled, obviously bothered by the fact that Bubbles knew about her upcoming birthday.

"You know what else?" Bubbles said.

Salamander didn't answer. Bubbles patiently accepted her silence with arms folded. Finally she looked up. "What, copper?"

"I've read in your file that there are a whole lot of people—intelligent people, even—who think you have Asperger's syndrome. But I don't think so."

"No?"

"No. For one thing, the *DSM-V* has now abandoned Asperger's as a distinct disorder. It's been enfolded into Autism, Not Otherwise Specified. But that's not the main thing. People think you're autistic because you have trouble forming bonds with other humans and can multiply four-digit numbers in your head. But that's only part of being autistic. People with autism have trouble making sense of human behavior; they can't understand the internal psychological states of others. You're not like that in the least. In fact, you're remarkably sharp and insightful in your dealings with others. You know exactly what's going on in the minds of those around you and can predict how someone will act with uncanny accuracy. You excel at strategic thinking."

"Is that a fact?"

"It is. Your problem, Fröken Salamander, isn't genetic, it's developmental. You're like a feral child, like Kaspar Hauser or the Wild Boy of Aveyron. You experienced early childhood traumas, and as a result you became a fiercely guarded person who won't let other people get close. Your guardedness was a perfectly rational response to traumas of your early life. Only now you don't know how to let the defenses down. You know only how to keep people at bay. Even people who want to be your friend."

"Cut the psychologizing, copper."

"I'm not trying to be clinical, Fröken. I'm just saying that I think I understand you. I also didn't have the happiest of childhoods. True, I never saw my mother beaten senseless, I wasn't buried alive by siblings, and I never immolated anyone in my immediate family. But I *was* placed under great pressure to study medicine, even though I had no interest in becoming a doctor. I know how these early childhood wounds can leave permanent scars."

"Okay, copper. Enough."

"It's all too easy to imagine: how a little girl, a *sensitive* little girl with intellectual gifts, who wants nothing more than to be loved by her *moder* and *fader*, instead witnesses terrible scenes, *awful* scenes, scenes no child should *ever* have to witness. How in order to *survive,* and not just anywhere, but in *Sweden,* she has to build elaborate defenses, ramparts of self-protection that permit her to function, but that also keep the world at a distance, lest anyone hurt her again, just as she was so grievously hurt as a little girl."

"*Stop!*"

Bubbles didn't push any further. But he noticed that while he was speaking, Salamander had made a number of increasingly tentative, even weak moves, first surrendering a pawn and then sacrificing position. She kept her eyes riveted on the board, but this didn't help, nor did her fifth Twinkie. In a dreadful, completely uncharacteristic blunder, she dropped her queen's bishop and three moves later resigned.

"Congratulations, copper. You managed to break my concentration. How would you like to celebrate your victory?"

"If you put it that way, Fröken Salamander. Would you be so kind as to remove your T-shirt and turn around?"

"You call that a modular sofa?" thundered Dagher Ukea.

The members of the sofa design team were gathered around a conference table in UKEA's top-secret underground design studio. Each had been frisked for smartphones, cameras, and other electronic equipment before entering the studio.

"I'm sorry, sir." The chief of sofa design turned deathly pale. The other seven members of his team trembled in their chairs.

"Sorry?" Ukea sprayed saliva. "This looks like something designed by Danish Inspirations!"

A member of the team quietly wept.

"No wonder we're losing market share," screamed Ukea. "Who'd want to sit in this sofa? Only a clinically obese American!"

"That is our target audience," ventured the sofa chief.

"No! That is not the way we do things at UKEA. What was Sløber's credo?"

" 'A sofa all can sit in,' " they called out in unison.

"What does *all* mean?"

" 'From a dainty Chinaman to a disgusting Texan'," they called out.

"Then why did you design this monstrosity?"

No one met Ukea's one-eyed glare.

"Let's hear from bed linen," he snapped.

A designer at the far end of the table cleared her throat. "Sir, as you know, this remains one of our more recent ventures. Obviously it takes time to establish a new product line. We're quite pleased with the progress that we've made with pillowcases and fitted bottom sheets. However—"

"Cut to the chase!"

"We're still getting killed in top sheets and duvet covers."

"Why?!"

"We're not entirely sure, sir. It appears that we're having trouble luring consumers away from Marimekko."

The mention of Marimekko brought silence to the room. All eyes turned to Ukea. He appeared to gyrate in his seat; his eye rolled briefly back in its socket, leaving only white exposed.

"*Never* . . ." he hissed.

"Yes, sir."

"EVER . . ."

"My deepest apologies, sir."

". . . mention *that* name in my presence."

"Rest assured, sir. It will never happen again."

"I know *you'll* never do it again. You're *fired*."

The designer accepted this stoically. Following firm protocol, she left her briefcase and papers at the table, stripped down to her panties and bra, and silently exited the conference room. In the twenty years of Ukea's run as CEO, no male senior staffer had ever been let go. In the same time, 788 female executives had been fired. Several more had simply gone missing.

"What's the word from countertops?" Ukea asked quietly.

All the news was bad. Wall panels, knobs and handles, curtain rods—everything was off. And it wasn't just the world economic downturn. The designs were awful, the materials cheap and the craftsmanship shoddy. Of course, this was all in keeping with Ukea's carefully elaborated long-term master plan. A couple of years before, Ukea had hired a team of American consultants recently released from federal prison. The team had prepared a secret report that concluded:

UKEA stands for quality at a reasonable cost. Market research suggests that we can trade on our reputation in order to raise the latter while cutting the former.

And so the Office of Quality Control was eliminated, Research and Development shut down, the design staff slashed by 90 percent, and all the master craftsmen were taken out to a field and shot. Only now, inconceivably, sales seemed to be suffering.

Just a week earlier, UKEA'S chief of corporate strategies had spoken with Ukea about possible responses to the downturn. "We could reverse, at least temporarily, the master plan."

"Meaning what?" demanded Ukea.

"Reduce prices and reintroduce quality control. Hire back some master carpenters."

"They're buried in a mass grave."

"We could kidnap some from Danish Inspirations."

"Impossible," snapped Ukea. "We must remain true to Sløber's credo."

"Just say no to Danes!" barked the chief of corporate strategy.

What Ukea hadn't mentioned was that even if the reversal strategy made sense, the money just wasn't there to implement it. Ukea was a fervent patriot, proud to be a Swede. He chaired an ultranationalist political group, Keep Sweden Safe for Xenophobes (SX). SX had a simple platform. Enough immigration! Enough foreign influence. Enough impossible languages and weird dress and exotic spices! *Finns out of Stockholm! Norwegians out of Uppsala!*

Ukea's passionate love of country did not, however, extend to Sweden's tax code. Over the years, he'd funneled billions of kronor to dozens of overseas dummy accounts set up in the Cayman Islands, Costa Rica, Andorra, Vanuatu, and Delaware. These accounts had been established under a number of personal aliases. The monies in these accounts had been used to pay for Ukea's basic living expenses, including the upkeep of his twenty-five yachts, fourteen palatial homes, three private jets, and a flotilla of decommissioned battleships. To cover the billions he removed from UKEA employees' pension fund, Ukea had invested the company's remaining cash in a complex network of foolproof exotic banking instruments whose reliability had been vouchsafed by a former chief of the US Federal Reserve, now serving concurrent life terms. All these investments were now worthless.

It might have been possible for Ukea to sell off his priceless art collection and downsize his fleet of yachts, but he didn't believe in private bailouts for public corporations. UKEA would have to dig itself out of its own hole, even if Ukea himself had been the prime earth mover. So the money to change course simply wasn't there.

Unless, of course, the cash came from the Swedish state. That at least would be an equitable solution. But the chances of getting a government bailout might not survive the scandal should the story of Little Adolf's role in founding the company ever hit the shelves. And now there was this Chamelea Salamander and Mikael Blomberg to worry about. He recalled the words of his father, Sløber: "Dagher, don't let problems snowball. Be proactive. Kill early and often."

Back in his office, he threw himself into his chair. His mastiffs sensed their master's displeasure. They whined miserably.

Ukea pressed a button on his office phone, summoning his secretary. "Anna, get my assassin on the phone."

Salamander removed her T-shirt and turned her back to Bubbles. She wore no bra.

"If you're planning to fuck my ass, copper, could you at least use some lube?"

"Fröken Salamander, please. Nothing could be further from my thoughts."

Salamander sighed. She should have felt relieved, but she didn't. Over the years, through painful practice, she'd learned not to let her abuser have the satisfaction of feeling his power. She'd learned to lock out the nasty, to travel to a faraway imaginary place

where army ants fed on the genitals of rapists, molesters, and pe-
dophiles.

But this Svenjamin Fucking Bubbles was something different.
He was far worse than Mikael Fucking Blomberg. Blomberg was
just a dick who fancied himself Mr. Sensitive. Bubbles was a Mind-
fuck. He was seriously screwing with her head.

It had started with the chess games and math puzzles. Salamander knew it was all a pathetically transparent copper ploy to
get her to talk, but it was still strangely effective. She'd started
looking forward to their games, and when he suddenly stopped
coming after Jessie went viral, Salamander had felt something
close to regret.

Deep down, she knew that he was just another fucking rancid
copper waiting for a chance to press stale Swedish kisses on her
death-black lips and drip molten wax on her muscular boyish buttocks. It was just a matter of time. In the meanwhile, she had to
find the goods on SFB. She'd hack into his computer, where she'd
find a stash of disgusting incriminating documents, a massive
trove of repulsive photos and gag-reflex-inducing film: the vicious
letters of blackmail; the reckless bank records making clear a sordid history of bribes and kickbacks; the sick emails describing little
girls stalked, colleagues menaced, prostitutes threatened; the vid-
eos documenting unspeakable acts of sexual slavery, spousal tor-
ment, and animal torture; the thousands of photos of drugged and
violated woman; and the detailed architectural plans of his own
private underground chamber of sadism and saturnalia.

Only they weren't there. She'd never come across such a boring
hard drive before. His desktop had all but put her to sleep. A file
promisingly titled "Kronor received" was filled with documents
from Bubbles's work as the treasurer of his synagogue. All contri-

butions were scrupulously listed. His checking account was balanced. His mortgage payments were modest and up-to-date. His library books were returned on time. His Volvo S40 FWD had recently had its oil changed and its tire pressure checked. Restaurant bills showed an interest in ethnic cuisine. He appeared to order vegetarian. Receipts indicated a taste for Dutch beer and Belgian chocolate. He belonged to a gym, but there was no record of anabolic steroid use. From Amåzön.se he'd recently bought a book called *Historic Thrusts*, but this turned out to be a study of King Gustavus Adolphus Magnus's bold military campaign in 1625 during the height of the Swedish-Polish war that resulted in the occupation of Livonia. He bought CDs of Edvard Grieg and Björk. He wore ECCO walking shoes. The only thing that caught her eye was an abundance of literature about Greenland, including a download of a learner's guide to Greenlandic, *Eskimo-Aleut Dialect in Twelve Easy Lessons*. But she could discover no trace of any secret dummy accounts in banks in downtown Nuuk.

Obviously Bubbles had preemptively cleaned up his computer. After all, the copper had already been burned by her world-class hacking skills. But then where was he hiding the dirt?

When Bubbles asked her to remove her T-shirt, Salamander had felt something bordering on glee. *Copper reveals his true colors.* But now he was back to playing his games. It was time to call his bluff. Salamander let her black cargo pants fall to the floor. She stepped out of her black panties. Naked except for her black knee socks, she turned to the inspector.

"Okay, copper. Go ahead. Fuck me. Just make it quick. There's a program about Amy Winehouse that I want to watch at 7 PM."

Bubbles gathered her panties and cargo pants and handed them back to her.

"Fröken Salamander, I fear you misunderstand my intentions."

Salamander grabbed Bubbles by the lapels of his blue and yellow police-issue blazer and threw him down on her bed. "I understand you all too clearly, copper. Now get to it. Fuck me."

Officer Snorkkle heard the telltale sounds of mortal skirmish coming from Salamander's cell. He raced in, gun drawn. The prisoner was straddling the chief inspector and violently thrashing him to and fro.

"Should I blow her head off, Chief?" asked Snorkkle.

"No, Officer," Bubbles gasped. "Everything's under control."

"Are you sure, Chief? Should I gather the hostage negotiating team?"

"Thank you, Officer. I'll be fine."

Snorkkle had never seen a naked prisoner work the chief over like that. He was reminded of a nature documentary on Swedish fauna he'd recently seen on TV 4 Fakta with dramatic footage of mating lynx. Reluctantly he withdrew. As he closed the door to the cell, he said, as if in an afterthought, "Hey, Cunt, you're not as flat-chested as I thought."

Salamander smiled.

When Bubbles recovered consciousness, Salamander was lying on her side, back to him, smoking.

"No cigarettes are permitted in gaol," said Bubbles.

"What are you going to do, copper? Arrest me?" Salamander laughed at her own joke, then turned toward Bubbles and growled.

Instinctively he flinched. Salamander laughed again.

"So, copper, do you make it a practice of fucking your inmates?"

"Funny, Fröken Salamander. I asked you to remove your T-shirt so I could examine the tattoos on your back."

"I'm sure that's the line you use on all your inmates after you fuck them. There must be rules against this kind of thing, copper."

"Please stop calling me that."

"If you stop this Fröken bullshit."

"Agreed. I shall call you Lizzy."

"And I'll call you . . . copper."

She settled her naked back against Bubbles and watched the rest of the docudrama about Amy Winehouse on her B&O flatscreen.

Bubbles traced the elaborate dinosaur tattoo on her muscular back with his forefinger.

"I've always wanted to visit Yale's Peabody Museum," he said.

"My father took me there when I was a child," said Salamander quietly. *Her moods turn rapidly.* "The KGB sent him to New Haven to strangle a CIA double agent. I got to spend two hours alone in the museum. I fell in love with the Zallinger mural."

"Of course, paleontologists now know that Tyrannosaurus didn't drag his tail," she continued. "He used it as a counterweight to aid his running. Apparently he was quite fast."

"And warm-blooded."

"Yes."

"But those weird little forearms are still a mystery."

"They might have been used for shredding. In close combat."

Bubbles surprised himself by placing a gentle kiss on the nape of Salamander's neck, where Velociraptor's severed leg peeked from Tyrannosaurus's mouth. And then said what they both knew. "No Baltic sturgeon."

"Nope."

"Why didn't you say something?"

"I don't talk to coppers."

"You were prepared to just sit here and let yourself get convicted for two murders that you never committed?"

She shrugged. "There are worse places than gaol. I have my mainframe and my Big Bill's and my Twinkies. What more can a girl ask for?"

"And the girl with the sturgeon tattoo. Do you have any idea who's trying to frame you?"

"Maybe."

"And?"

"And nothing. You seem to forget. I don't talk to coppers. Even ones I fuck."

Bubbles sighed. "You know, Fröken—I mean, Lizzy—the fact is, I have information that even you don't have."

"Good work, copper."

"Only it doesn't involve the Arssen murder or the girl with the sturgeon tattoo. I believe that shortly before your arrest, you were doing some research on the murder of a pregnant reindeer whose body was found downtown."

Salamander turned toward Bubbles. "That's right. Have you made an arrest?"

"No. But we have a suspect. A suspect of great interest to you."

Salamander frowned. "And who might that be?"

"Lizzy, we must try to help each other."

"I don't need anyone's help."

"Suit yourself." Bubbles gathered his chess set and book of MENSA puzzles. As he was about to leave the cell, he turned back and glanced at Salamander. She was still naked, curled on her side, watching her program. *Perhaps it would be possible to redo the tattoo so that the Tyrannosaurus isn't dragging his tail.* He felt for her. Why, he didn't know, but he did.

"It's the identical twin of your half brother. The one you stapled to that barn ceiling."

Salamander's eyes widened. Then she said, "I don't talk to coppers. Ever. But ask your friend Blomberg about the Baltic sturgeon girl. Maybe he can tell you something."

TEN

LÖRDAG, FEBRUARI 12–MÅNDAG, FEBRUARI 14

Thirty-two percent of Nobel Laureates in Economics have been convicted of sex crimes. This compares to 21% of Laureates in Literature, 18% of those for Peace, and 12% of those in Physics.
—HAMPUS THORKILL, WOUNDED WINNERS: THE NOBEL PRIZE
1901–2001 *(STOCKHOLM: FOGWHORN & KLOV, 2005)*

Blomberg sat in the rectangular main reading room of the UKEA corporate archive. An archivist silently approached him on slippered feet. Her hair was pinned back severely, but it wasn't the same archivist who had helped him last time. Her name tag identified her as Humida Chiklett.

"What happened to your colleague with the different-colored eyes?"

"I'm afraid she's no longer with us," said the new archivist. "Not everyone can cope with the stresses of the job."

Blomberg glanced around the entirely empty reading room. Just as in his last visit, four additional archivists were stationed at each corner, watching them intently. But these four faces were also new.

"Would you be so kind as to bring me the file on a former employee? Her name is Chamelea Salamander."

At the mention of the name all the archivists began coughing violently.

"You must fill out a form," said Ms. Chiklett, having regained her breath.

Carefully Blomberg filled out the request and signed the nondisclosure form at the bottom.

"What is the name?" said Ms. Chiklett, examining the request.

"Chamelea Salamander."

The coughing resumed.

"I cannot make it out." The archivist tore the request in quarters. "Please, try again. And more legibly."

Blomberg wrote CHAMELEA SALAMANDER in gradeschool block letters.

The archivist examined the letters carefully, sighed, and disappeared into the stacks.

She returned two hours later with a large file. It contained a pile of ashes. Blomberg touched them. Still warm.

"Might there be anything on Salamander that hasn't just been incinerated?" Blomberg asked.

"I can check." The archivist disappeared into the stacks and returned an hour later.

"I'm afraid that was all the material we have for the requested name."

"I see."

As Blomberg handed the pile of ashes back to the archivist, their hands briefly touched. A soft moan escaped Ms. Chiklett's lips.

"You're Mikael Blomberg, aren't you?" she whispered.

"That's correct."

The archivist removed the pins from her hair. Brunette curls cascaded to her shoulders. All at once Blomberg recognized Ms. Chiklett. She had been a former Olympic silver medalist in the giant slalom before going on to become Fröken Universe 2006. As she stepped out of her archivist's jumpsuit, Blomberg admired her beautiful toned body. *These former Fröken Universes stay in excellent shape.*

She helped Blomberg out of his clothes.

"Here?" he asked.

"They won't notice," she whispered. With a broad motion she swept the pile of ashes off the table and lay down, legs parted. The other archivists appeared to be watching closely.

"Are you sure the table can support our weight?" asked Blomberg. His plan to cut back on the fried eel hadn't exactly been successful.

"Ordinarily I would say yes," said Chiklett. "Only this table was made by UKEA." Together they laughed.

The archivist was a tender and imaginative lover. It was clear she had spent her childhood on a farm surrounded by wolfhounds.

After they were done, Blomberg lit a cigarette.

Chiklett gently touched his lips. "Excuse me, sir. Smoking is strictly forbidden in the UKEA Corporate Archive. We wouldn't want our documents to suffer any mishaps, would we?" She glanced mischievously at the torched material scattered on the floor.

Blomberg, however, had turned pensive. "Humida, I want you to give me an honest answer. I'm forty-seven years old, thick across the middle. My digestive tract rumbles and my knees creak.

My gums are receding, as is my hairline. I reek of stale cigarettes, my burps smell like yesterday's coffee, and my teeth are the color of meatballs. My best writing was done years ago. Now I'm stuck writing a blog that no one reads and taking assignments from crackpots. Why do women, beautiful women, accomplished women, why do they find me irresistible?"

"Because you're cute," she said, planting a kiss on his nose.

"But I'm *not*. Not in the least. I mean, come on, I'm not exactly Daniel Craig. I'm dumpy and middle-aged. Sometimes I think I'm living someone else's fantasy of being a chick magnet. As if my whole life were just some loser's projection of what it would feel like to be wildly successful with women. Does that make any sense?"

Chiklett had nodded off. Blomberg watched her sleep. When she woke up, they had sex again. In the throes of passion, she whispered in his ear, to avoid being overheard by the other archivists, "There was more. In the stacks."

"About Chamelea?"

She nodded.

"Can you bring it to me?"

"I don't think so. But if you slip me your iPad, I could photograph everything."

"iPads don't have cameras."

"Damn. I forgot."

"My iPhone has a camera, though."

"Good. Slip it to me very nonchalantly so the others don't notice. I'll need to keep it hidden."

"Where should I put it?"

"Use your imagination."

———

They drove in Blomberg's '07 Volvo S60 AWD to the shågshäck on Lake Fikmisst. They stopped twice during the 100-kilometer trip, first when the "check engine light" went on, and then again when the brakes caught on fire.

Humida lay naked on the bed reading the newest thriller by Henning Mankell.

"Is it any good?" asked Blomberg.

Humida shook her head. "Garbage. But it passes the time."

Blomberg built a fire, using a copy of *BLINK!* for kindling. He was still sent copies of the magazine gratis. He glanced at the table of contents. *Björn Borg's Gray Hair: dignified or just old-looking? Princess Victoria's Meatballs: BLINK! reveals the secret ingredient.* He tossed it into the fireplace. It didn't even burn well.

"Are you comfortable?" he asked.

"It's so cozy. Though you could use a few more pillows. UKEA does an attractive reindeer-motif pillow that would look nice on the bed."

"I thought those were reserved for employees with more than ten years' service."

"True, but I think some are available on eBay."

They fell silent.

Blomberg went outside to chop down a towering pinetree for firewood. It was a brisk −60 degrees. He took off his flannel shirt and tied it around his waist. After a few whacks he was exhausted and sweating profusely. As he rested against his axe, he thought he noticed movement in the woods near his shack. *Probably just a gigantic bear with blond hair.* He took a few more halfhearted whacks and returned to his cabin carrying a modest pile of twigs.

Humida looked up from her book admiringly. "So few Swedish men have real love handles," she said.

Blomberg was about to begin examining the jpegs of the Chamelea file on his Expedia Droid FX45 MOnstER when "Take a Chance on Me" chimed. He'd recently changed his ringtone. He told people the ABBA was meant ironically, but in fact he liked the song.

"Blomberg here."

"Mikael."

"Hi, Erotikka. I was about to call you . . ."

"Oh, Mikael. Didn't we promise each other never to lie? Tell me, who is she?"

Blomberg could recall no such promise. He glanced at Humida. She was trimming her pubic hair into the shape of a heart. "Sweetheart, there's no one else, I swear."

"Where are you?"

"Still at the dentist."

Erotikka sighed. "When will I see you?"

"Soon. I promise."

"But *when?*"

All at once Blomberg lost his patience. "I don't *know* when. To be honest, Humida Chiklett, the former Fröken Universe, is lying naked on my bed, on the very UKEA rabbit and eel pattern sheets *you* picked out. Do I feel guilty about having had sex with her twelve times in the last day? Not in the least. It's you who should feel guilty for badgering me and behaving impossibly. Honestly, I don't know what's gotten into you. If you *truly* cared about me, you'd know that it's crucial for my self-esteem to have as many meaningless sexual encounters as possible. Having anonymous sex helps me forget that I live in a tiny country with an atrocious climate full of tall, untalkative people. It's that or drinking myself to death. If you want to get all hysterical over monogamous love, I suggest you go to America."

"Oh, Mikael. I'm *so* sorry, you're absolutely right. You're the most sensitive man I've ever met. I love you so."

"And I like you a great deal, Erotikka. Sex with you helps me to cope with the weather forecast. But it creates nothing in the way of obligations. To the contrary."

"I understand completely."

"Now I have to get back to work. Send my regards to Ralf."

"And mine to Humida. I remember when she won in 2006. We were all so proud."

Blomberg examined Chamelea Salamander's UKEA file. Two things stood out. She'd quickly established herself as a talented young designer of everything from napkin rings to seat cushions. At the end of her first year, she received an excellent evaluation from her corporate mentor. *Salamander is creative, focused, and a team player. With the proper tutelage she could easily advance to tables and bookcases, and perhaps to dressers. She's a keeper.* A year later, the tenor of her mentor's report was altogether different. *Subject terminated.* That same month, she was institutionalized. The doctor responsible for her evaluation was Madder Telepathian, the same psychiatrist who'd once testified against Lizzy and who'd also authorized Odder Arssen's institutionalization. The file made clear that Telepathian tried a variety of treatments on Salamander, none of which proved effective. And yet all at once, without a word of explanation in the file, she was released from the asylum.

It's time we paid a visit to Dr. Telepathian. Ever since Lizzy had begun hacking into his brain, he often found himself thinking in the royal we.

———

Dr. Madder Telepathian's office was in Sluttersholm, a neighborhood in Stockholm popular with dotcommers, Helsinki ex-pats, and members of the Lithuanian underworld.

"Please, come in." The doktor ushered Blomberg into his office with ten-foot ceilings. Telepathian indicated that Blomberg should recline on the UKEA self-assembly Jung psychoanalytic couch patterned with signs of the universal unconscious.

"I'm not here as a patient," said Blomberg.

"You're not the first to say that," responded Dr. Telepathian. The psychiatrist was six foot four but a willowy 175 pounds. Blomberg guessed his age as sixty-three. He had pale skin, a thin tapered beard, and red pupils that made Blomberg uneasy.

"We've met before," said Blomberg.

"Yes, I recall. You testified against me at Lizzy Salamander's trial. You claimed that I had falsified my report recommending civil commitment for the remainder of her natural life."

"Your report *was* falsified."

"An interpretation. But rest assured, Mr. Blomberg, I hold no grudges. Admittedly I experienced some personal and professional difficulties as a result of that trial. I was exposed as a fraud, an extremist, and the owner of the largest collection of child pornography in Western Europe. My private practice collapsed and my talk show on Radio3, *Ask Doktor Telepathian,* was abruptly canceled. But I feel I have gained from the experience. I published a memoir. Perhaps you might discuss it in your blog."

He handed Blomberg a copy of *Healer, Heal Thyself. How a Leading Psychiatrist Confronted His Own Sadism, Pedophilia, and Neo-Nazism.* Blomberg rifled through the book. There were many pictures of a younger, more dashing Telepathian posing next to restrained patients.

"Please, it's yours to keep. Your readers might be interested to learn that I've found great strength in Norse mythology."

Blomberg noticed the small rune hanging around the doktor's neck.

"I take it, however, that you're not here to discuss my remarkable comeback. And from your note, I gather that you're not here to talk about Lizzy Salamander, either."

"No, I'm interested in her twin sister, Chamelea."

"Fraternal, as I remember."

"That's right."

A smile crossed Telepathian's face as he mused aloud. "Strange that I should be responsible for the institutionalization of two such different twins. And yet I suppose I've been responsible for institutionalizing many of our fellow Swedes over the last thirty years. And, a great number of our Estonian neighbors."

"How were they different, Lizzy and Chamelea?"

"I met Lizzy at a much earlier point in her life. As a twelve-year-old girl she displayed a classic combination of intermittent explosive disorder, pyromania, antisocial personality disorder, sexual aversion disorder, schizoaffective disorder, transvestic fetishism, and vaginismus. She was quite good at chess, though."

"And Chamelea?"

"She suffered from what we call grandiose delusional disorder."

"From her file it appears that you tried numerous therapies."

"Correct. At first I hoped the patient would respond to a combination of drug and behavioral therapy."

"It indicates here that you prescribed Risperdal, Seroquel, Zyprexa, fluphenazine, and Pimozide, first separately and then in combination in daily psychotropic cocktails."

"Sadly, there was little by way of increased lucidity."

"Next you tried electroconvulsive therapy, lobotomy, and forced sterilization."

"Here again the patient showed less than desired improvement."

"You then moved on to stress positions, sleep deprivation, and waterboarding."

"The efficacy was not what we hoped for."

"What exactly were her symptoms?"

"You must understand, Mr. Blomberg, that when Chamelea Salamander began work at UKEA, she scored a Normal Plus on the Scandinavian Workers' Diagnostic Exam, the highest score possible. Not only was she a talented and an imaginative designer, but she was an exceptionally happy and well-adjusted employee. In her first year alone, she received ten monthly ☺s, an unheard-of total.

"Then in her second year, something suddenly changed. Chamelea announced that she was bringing a lawsuit against UKEA. Members of Ukea's senior management—many of whom, to be frank, suffer from bipolar disorder with psychotic features—assumed this would be a typical sexual harassment suit and responded according to the procedures listed in UKEA's bylaws. They planted thousands of messages on Salamander's office computer purporting to show that she'd performed circus-like sex acts on all her subordinates.

"Only Fröken Salamander's suit was of an altogether different nature. She claimed that she was entitled to a share in *all* of UKEA's profits. She claimed that she owned a propriety interest in UKEA's original designs, going all the way back to the creation of the firm in the 1940s."

"But she had only joined the firm in 2004."

"Correct. And had only been responsible for the design of one popular shower curtain and two napkin rings."

"That does sound crazy."

"As a doktor, I prefer 'deranged.' But the story is not over. Fröken Salamander never claimed that she was personally responsible for UKEA's early designs. Instead, she claimed that her family, such as it is, owns the rights, because she believed her grandfather was responsible for UKEA's original designs."

"Well, who was her grandfather?"

"I'm afraid here is where the delusions take a turn to the grandiose. Fröken Chamelea Salamander insisted that her grandfather was Adolf Hitler." Doktor Telepathian could not suppress a giggle. "Deranged, no?"

"It certainly sounds crazy," Blomberg said. "And yet Odder Arssen also claimed that Hitler made the sketches that Ukea used for his first furniture line."

"Ah, Odder Arssen. Another incurable schizophrenic. Certainly you give no credence to these sad fantasies, Mr. Blomberg. Because if you do, there are several medications that could prove of help."

Doktor Telepathian quickly wrote out some words on a sheet of medical stationery and handed it to Blomberg. *Haloperidol 20 mg b.i.d.* "There's a pharmacy down the street. I'll call in the prescription."

"Thank you. But if Chamelea Salamander was so incurably sick why was she released barely a year later?"

"Ah, an excellent question. Here I'm afraid we encounter a sad example of law winning out over medical science. The advokats for UKEA, many of whom I would like to see medicated and institutionalized for Acute Stress Disorder, worked out a nonsuit agreement with Fröken Salamander's advokat. Under the terms of this agreement, UKEA promised to deinstitutionalize Fröken Salamander in return for her voluntary waiver of her right to sue."

"And she signed?"

"Yes. I believe largely thanks to the urging of her advokat, a woman with tendencies to agoraphobic panic disorder. But even after the agreement was signed and the patient was about to be released, she continued to claim that she was Hitler's granddaughter. She never stopped insisting this."

"Do you happen to remember who her lawyer was?"

"Her name was Anoraka Giardia. Perhaps you know her."

"She's my sister."

"Indeed. She made life quite difficult for me when she represented Lizzy Salamander. But that's a different story, isn't it? And as I've said, I hold no grudges."

Blomberg drove home in his Volvo S60 AWD. He stopped once along the way to replace a defective timing belt. As he turned onto Bellmansgatan, he noticed something peculiar. Driving the opposite direction was an enormous man in a black Smart Car. The man was so large that his head protruded from the open cloud-roof. He appeared oblivious to the heavy snow that had covered much of his face and the icicles hanging from his ears. Blomberg and the man exchanged glances as their cars passed on the narrow street. *Odd. He looks exactly like . . . But, no. Impossible.*

Blomberg returned to his 905-square-foot attic apartment to find it ransacked. The intruder had stolen his MacBook Pro with 2.53 GHz Inter Core 2 Duo Processor, but nothing else appeared to be missing. Still, that hadn't stopped the intruder from thoroughly trashing the place. Socks and underwear had been tossed on the floor, shirts pulled from their hangers, pencils split in half. Even the DVDs from Blomberg's Criterion Collection of the films of Ingmar Bergman had been flung about the living room. He instinctively examined the DVD of *The Seventh Seal*. Scratched. A slow rage percolated within Blomberg.

On his iPhone, he texted Bubbles.

<This might sound strange, but I think Ronni Niemand has risen from the dead. That, or he's been cloned. In either case, I believe he just robbed my apartment.>

Bubbles's answer came promptly.

<It's time we compared notes.>

They met at Yngve's, a new kaffeklinik popular with the twentysomething software designers from Egidii. Blomberg drank Guevara's Organic Anti-imperialist Roast from a twenty-liter aquarium. Chief Inspector Bubbles sipped peppermint tea.

"Let's dispense with the charades," said the inspector.

"Agreed."

"So what have you got? I know that Fröken Salamander's not the girl with the sturgeon tattoo."

"Actually it *is* Salamander, only not Lizzy. It's her fraternal twin sister, Chamelea."

Bubbles took this in. "I didn't even know Fröken Salamander had a sister, least of all a twin."

"Lizzy never talks about her, not that Lizzy ever talks about much of anything. They never got along, even when they were little. Now they're entirely estranged."

"Evidently so. She tried to frame her sister for the murder of an unpublished writer. What did Chamelea Salamander have against Arssen? And Ekkrot, for that matter?"

"Here's where the story gets complicated. I told you that Arssen's father believes that Twig was working on a book that claimed Hitler was responsible for UKEA's early designs, such as its popular Über Alles line of matching bedroom furniture. Arssen believes Twig may have been murdered to stop him from publishing. Certainly UKEA would have powerful incentive to make sure Twig's book never hit the shelves. I was able to learn that Chamelea Salamander worked for UKEA for a number of years. Everything seemed clear. Dagher Ukea had hired Chamelea to find the manuscript and to kill Twig. Only then I discovered that Chamelea despises Dagher and the company. A number of years ago, she brought a lawsuit against the firm, alleging that she was entitled to hundreds of millions of kronor in royalties, as a descendant of UKEA's original designer."

"But according to Arssen, the original designer was Hitler."

"Exactly. Chamelea insists that Hitler was her grandfather."

"Remarkable. What became of the lawsuit?"

"Chamelea dropped the suit as a quid pro quo for being released from UKEA's asylum for criminally insane employees. She'd been institutionalized as soon as she filed the lawsuit. The psychiatrist responsible for her civil commitment was Madder Telepathian."

"Ah, the same psychiatrist who testified against Lizzy and Odder Arssen. From what I recall, Telepathian just published a memoir of his struggle to overcome pedophilia and neo-Nazism."

"Yes, it's on my nightstand. He wants me to plug it in my blog."

"If Chamelea Salamander isn't working for Ukea, then who *is* she working for?"

"A good question. Maybe herself. If she can prove the family connection to Hilter and if Twig's manuscript proves Hitler's connection to UKEA, then Twig's book would be incredibly valuable to her."

"True. But why decapitate him? Why not just let him publish? And why kill Ekkrot? How does he fit in?"

"I don't know. Maybe she came to Twig asking to see the manuscript and he refused. He was always very secretive. Maybe he died trying to protect his manuscript."

"And Ekkrot?"

"He was Twig's closest friends from Royal Tennis Academy days. Maybe Chamelea thought Ekkrot was hiding the manuscript for Twig. This is all speculation."

"Do you think Chamelea has the manuscript? In the murder video it's clear that she found Twig's laptop."

"According to Twig's father, Twig used his computer only to blog. He typed everything on an old Hermes manual."

"Like Peter Høeg."

"Exactly."

"Which means Chamelea must still be searching for it."

"Yes."

"And Ukea?"

"I suspect that he's eager to find Twig's manuscript, too."

Just then an attractive woman of forty at the next table turned to them. "Pardon me, but I couldn't help but overhear your entire conversation. It's just fascinating. It sounds like something straight out of a Swedish thriller."

Bubbles discreetly flashed her his police identification. "Ma'am, we can't comment on official business. It's confidential."

The woman nodded but appeared not to have heard Bubbles. Her foam green eyes were focused on Blomberg. "Are you by any chance . . . ?"

"I am."

The woman quickly wrote down a phone number and a short message. She passed it to him under the table. *If you ever want some distraction from the Baltic climate . . .*

She left the kaffeklinik staring longingly back over her shoulder.

Bubbles sipped his peppermint tea. Blomberg drained the last of his aquarium of espresso.

"Would you like to split an order of fried eel?" Blomberg asked.

"No, but you go ahead and order. Maybe I'll have a bite."

Blomberg placed the order while Bubbles described what he had learned.

"The seven-foot giant insensible to cold whom you saw in the Smart Car was not the second coming of Ronni Niemand. It was Niemand's identical twin brother, Reinhard. In contrast to the Salamander twins, it appears that the two Niemands were quite close. They grew up in Leipzig, later moved to Berlin after the wall came down. Reinhard trained to become a chef, but his genetic disease made him vulnerable to inadvertently boiling off his skin and lighting himself on fire. Like his twin brother, he did some minor work for his father—mostly shipping weapons to Iceland and strangling prostitutes. Since his father's murder and his brother's death by stapling, he seems to have drifted around. His IQ is subpar and his education minimal. His native tongue is German and his Swedish remains mediocre. He's barely conversational in Dutch, Russian, and Polish, and has only a reading knowledge of French, Spanish, and Italian. I'd consider him just a typical petty thug except that we have firm evidence linking him to the recent reindeer slayings."

"What kind of evidence?"

"A pinkie that he must have accidentally severed at the site of the last killing. The DNA matched and the pinkie was enormous."

"But Niemand hardly fits the profile of a typical Reindeer Ripper."

"Exactly. All along I had assumed that the Arssen/Ekkrot de-capitations and the reindeer eviscerations were unrelated crimes. But as soon as Niemand emerged as a suspect, I started to have doubts. What you've told me about Chamelea makes me all the more certain that the crimes are connected. You see, after he dropped out of culinary art school, Reinhard Niemand worked briefly as a carpenter at UKEA's facility in Hamburg. And now there's this business about the robbery at your apartment. My investigators"—here Bubbles swallowed hard at the thought of Officer Flunk gathering evidence—"have examined your apart-ment and found a little something that should be able to tell us for sure whether Reinhard Niemand was responsible for the break-in. If so, that would prove a connection. You haven't been pursuing the reindeer case without my knowledge, have you?"

"Most certainly not."

"So you must have gotten on Niemand's radar as a result of your research into Arssen, UKEA, and Chamelea Salamander."

"But why break into my apartment?"

"Maybe he thought you'd found Twig's manuscript."

"Do you think he's working in tandem with his half sister?"

"That would be my assumption. But, again, it's just a guess."

"And the reindeer? How do they fit in?"

"Another mystery. Maybe the killings are meant to serve as a diversion. I don't know."

"And what about the missing manuscript?"

"By the sound of it, no one has found it. It must still be out there somewhere."

"And Lizzy?" Blomberg asked.

"We formally dropped the murder charges. We could have re-arrested her for illegally accessing protected data, but decided it wasn't worth the headache. Technically speaking she's a free woman, though her mainframe is still in her detention cell, as is most of her wardrobe and workout equipment. So she's been spending her nights there. She seems pretty . . . comfortable."

Only then did Blomberg notice his friend's black eyes and the bite marks on his forehead. Blomberg didn't push the matter further except to say, "Maybe we should have a talk with Lizzy. See if she can clear any of this up."

"I want that manuscript!"

"*Jawohl,* master!" The heavily accented voice on the phone was strangely high-pitched and squeaky.

"Then find it!"

"*Jawohl!*"

"And what about you-know-who, have you strangled her?"

"On my to-do list, *Meister!*"

"And Blomberg?"

"Reinhard almost strangle him yesterday."

"What happened?"

"It become dark."

Ukea rubbed a line of cocaine into his gums from several grams that he kept at the ready in his desktop UKEA pen case. *An assassin afraid of the dark. Who speaks bad Swedish.* His mood continued to darken.

"Moron."

"Yes, master."

"Have you read the afternoon paper?"

"Only *Fussball* results, master."

"The police have named you a person of interest in the ongoing investigation of a series of reindeer slayings and in the break-in of journalist Mikael Blomberg's apartment. How did they manage to link you to these incidents?"

"Reinhard do not know, *Meister*."

"You didn't happen to lose anything or leave anything behind at these crimes scenes, did you?"

"*Nein.*"

"Reinhard, how many fingers do you presently have?"

Ukea listened as Niemand counted over the phone. "*Eins, zwei, drei, vier, fünf, sechs* . . . six and one half, master. Almost seven."

"Didn't you have eight when we last spoke?"

There was silence on the line.

"Reinhard, did you lose another finger? And maybe a nail, too? And did you by chance leave these behind?"

"It is possible, *Meister*."

Ukea jabbed a hypodermic into his thigh and injected a speedball into his inferior vena cava. At last the sixty-year-old's nerves began to steady. He thought soberly, *My assassin is turning into a major liability. Niemand's capture would lead straight back to me, and that would be that. I'd have no choice but to resign as CEO of UKEA and maybe even give up my memberships on the board of Volvo and H&M.* That was to be avoided at all costs. He recalled the advice from his father, Sløber Ukea. "Son, at times you must assassinate the assassin." Yes. But not yet.

"I *need* that manuscript."

"Reinhard understand, master."

"And Reinhard—try not to lose any more fingers."

"*Jawohl, Meister!*"

ELEVEN

TISDAG, FEBRUARI 15–TISDAG, FEBRUARI 22

In the year 961, a bold band of Swedish virgins disguised themselves as men and established the Queendom of Gandalfa, a gynaecocracy ruled by Frigga the Ample. The brutal Viking King Harald Notooth soon caught wind of the ascension of the virgins. Leading a force of ten thousand sex-starved warriors, he attacked Gandalfa, slaughtering its citizens and suppressing its history forever.
—WHEN FRIGGA RULED (*HISTORY CHANNEL DOCUDRAMA*)

Blomberg and Bubbles entered Lizzy's cell. She was just finishing her morning exercises: one hour of core synergistics followed by ninety minutes each of targeted commando ball squats, hamstring curls, tuck leaps, box jumps, lateral thrusts, commando dips, shoulder-blade turbo push-ups, and tricep kickbacks. She powered down with thirty minutes of Kenpo ergo rips.

Her hair was pulled back in a ponytail. She hadn't dyed her hair since entering gaol, and now her red roots were clearly visible. Bubbles couldn't help but think of Pippi Longstocking, but knew better than to say anything. The stitches from the wound to his chin had been removed only the day before.

"Hello, Lizzy."

Salamander barely nodded. "Hello, Inspector. Hello, KFB."

Bubbles knew that Salamander liked to call Blomberg Kalle. But where did the F come from? *Thought his middle name was Solomon.*

Bubbles cleared his throat. "Lizzy, Mikael and I have pooled our information, and would like to ask you a few questions. If you don't mind."

The inspector noticed that Salamander was uneasy in Blomberg's presence. She avoided his eyes and kept thrusting her exercise bayonet at the face of a dummy marked *KFB*.

"We know that Arssen was killed by your sister. We believe her motive had something to do with a manuscript that Arssen was working on."

"About UKEA and *der Führer*?"

Bubbles mouth fell open. How could Salamander possibly know that? Bubbles had specifically avoided recording his conversation with Blomberg on his computer or iPhone. He hadn't even typed up a summary out of fear that any electronic file, no matter how securely protected or encrypted, could be compromised. They'd even bypassed Blomberg's cerebrum out of suspicion that Salamander had learned to hack into his brain. Yet still she knew.

"What can you tell us about your family's history?"

"You mean, do I believe Adolf Hitler was my grandfather?"

Again Salamander was two steps ahead of the game. "Any information about your family's past might be helpful, Lizzy. We know this topic isn't the easiest for you."

"My father"—it was the first time that Bubbles and Blomberg had ever heard her use this word in association with Kalashnikov— "rarely spoke about his own father. But every now and then he would make some comment, usually very vague. I remember him saying how hard it was for him to feel good about his own achievements as an assassin given that *his* father had been the greatest mass murderer in recorded history. Father said that everything he did seemed so trivial by comparison."

Bubbles and Blomberg glanced at each other. Neither had expected such candor on Salamander's part.

"Please go on."

"At times Father would get terribly drunk and would wallow in self-pity. I remember him once going on that Opa—that's what he called his father—had shot himself in the mouth and had ordered his body burned out of disappointment with his son. 'If only I hadn't been such an underachiever, Opa would be alive today!'

"I distinctly remember my mother telling father that that was ridiculous. That Opa—had killed himself to avoid capture by twenty million soldiers representing the collective military force of the entire civilized world. It had nothing to do with being let down by his son. My father never accepted this."

"Did your parents ever mention Hitler by name?"

"No, I would have remembered that. In fact, Chamelea and I used to argue. She was convinced Opa was Hitler. I thought he was Stalin. I was so . . . naïve."

"Why naïve? After all, your father grew up in the Soviet Union and worked for the KGB."

"True. And to my five-year-old mind it just didn't make sense that Hitler's son could become a Soviet agent. But later I looked into the history and chronology, why I don't know. The whole thing made me depressed. Hitler or Stalin—neither sounded good."

"When was your father born?"

"Nineteen thirty-five. He was fifty-six when Chamelea and I were born. But still quite energetic."

"So the chronology is possible. From what I recall, no historian has every been able to prove that Hitler had any children, though many claims of paternity have surfaced over the years."

"Which is why I focused my research on my father's mother. Her name was Herta Gebärmutter."

"Gebärmutter. That sounds vaguely familiar. Didn't she appear as the goddess of teutonic beauty in early Leni Riefenstahl films?"

"Yes! She was a beauty and was courted by many leading Nazis. When she gave birth in 1935 the SS rumor mill had its fill. Goebbels wrote in his diary, 'The adorable infant boy has fierce eyes, dark hair parted on the side, and a mole on his upper lip that looks distinctly like a little mustache.' Then Herta disappeared, only to surface in Moscow in 1936."

"She'd been a spy."

"Apparently she'd been working for the KGB all along. Having Hitler's child in the Kremlin was considered an astonishing coup, especially if he could be raised as a model Soviet citizen. Unfortunately Father turned into a model psychopath. With low self-esteem."

Bubbles had followed Salamander's story with astonishment. Blomberg looked equally amazed, both by the details and by Salamander's frankness. It was the first time he'd ever heard her string together consecutive sentences that weren't threats. But now she appeared exhausted and depressed by the ordeal of talking. "Quite a family, huh?" she said.

Bubbles gently rubbed her shoulders.

Not a good idea, thought Blomberg.

"Please don't do that," said Salamander.

"So what do you think?" asked Blomberg. "All said and done, do you believe the story is true?"

"I don't know what the fuck to think," said Salamander quietly.

Bubbles slipped her a Twinkie. This she accepted.

"We also believe that your twin sister might be working with your half brother, Reinhard Niemand. And that the reindeer killings are related to the search for Arssen's manuscript. What do you make of that?"

Salamander shrugged.

"Come, Lizzy. You've helped us to this point. Just these last few questions. No point in withdrawing into your 'Go fucking figure it out for yourself, Kalle Fucking Blomberg' mode."

Bubbles was surprised to hear Blomberg talk to Salamander in this way, though now he knew what the F stood for. He expected her to crush Blomberg's nose. Instead she sighed. "Chamelea and Reinhard Niemand? I just don't see it."

"Why not?"

"The Niemands once visited us for Christmas. Chamelea and I must have been eight. They were so big and rambunctious and always bleeding over everything. I remember Reinhard destroyed Chamelea's wooden Brio pull toy of Santa's sleigh. She cried and cried and told on Reinhard. Father was furious and made Reinhard sit outside in a blizzard during Christmas dinner. At breakfast the next morning, Reinhard tried to strangle her."

"If Chamelea and Niemand aren't working together, then who is Niemand working for?" Blomberg asked.

Only to answer his own question. "Ukea."

———

Moments later Officer Snorkkle burst into the cell. "Two more reindeer killings, sir."

"What can you tell me about the victims?"

"The first: mature female, large rack." Snorkkle glanced dismissively at Salamander's breasts; she gave him the finger. "The second: mature male, white spotting on chest."

"Where did the killings take place?"

"The first in downtown Rättvik. The second in the Fulu mountains."

"When?"

"According to Svenssen in Reindeer at the Institute, the murders took place almost exactly at the same time. Around noon yesterday."

"But Rättvik is at least a two-hour drive from the Fulus. Without traffic."

"And that's not the only strange thing, sir. The female in Rättvik was strangled, but not the male in the Fulus. He was decapitated."

"Were both eviscerated?"

"Yes, sir."

"Anything else?"

"Part of an index finger was found at the Rättvik crime scene."

"Thank you, Officer."

Snorkkle turned to Salamander. "I've been having trouble with my Plants vs. Zombies app."

"Bring it by this afternoon, Pigfuck."

"Great! Thanks."

As soon as the officer left the cell, Bubbles, Blomberg, and Salamander exchanged glances.

"Now Niemand and Chamelea are both killing reindeer," said Blomberg. "Are you *sure* they're not working together?"

"I'd be prepared to bet your life," said Salamander.

Blomberg found the formulation unsettling.

"If Niemand and Chamelea are supposed to be searching for Twig's manuscript," said Bubbles, "why are they spending all this time killing reindeer?"

"Maybe it's time for me to talk to Twig's father again," said Blomberg.

Blomberg met Nix Arssen in KaffeKultur, a new espresso bar in Skeppsholmen that catered to the posh Örnsköldsvik publishing crowd. Arssen appeared to have aged in recent weeks. The tip of his nose had turned black, a sure sign of frostbite. It had been a long winter.

"How is the search for Chamelea Salamander and my son's manuscript proceeding?" Arssen sounded fatigued, as if he no longer expected much from Blomberg.

"We're making steady progress."

"We?"

"Me and my tapeworm."

Arssen did not laugh at Blomberg's effort at levity.

"But I need to ask you a few more questions," Blomberg continued. "Did Twig have any special interests in reindeer?"

Arssen glanced at Blomberg suspiciously. "What are you trying to suggest?"

"Nothing at all. But it may be important."

"We all know that Twig had his trouble with women. But with reindeer? No. Never."

"During his childhood was Twig unusually interested in reindeer?"

"No more so than your average Swedish boy."

"You've told me before that Twig was anything but your average Swedish boy."

"True. But when it came to reindeer, Twig really was quite ordinary. He took riding lessons in school like everyone else and was quite good in the saddle, though never liked jumping."

"You said that Twig wrote a number of unpublished thrillers before his final manuscript."

"Yes, at least three. Three unsuccessful efforts."

"Do you have any idea where these might be?"

"Of course. I have them at my house. I planned to use them for kindling, but I never got around to it."

"Might I take a look at them?"

"Certainly, but why?"

"Do you happen to know Nicolas Cage, the American actor?"

"Yes. I remember him vividly in *Moonstruck,* a touching portrayal of the Italian-American experience."

"Well, several of Cage's more recent movies, including the box-office hit *National Treasure: Book of Secrets,* suggest that writers often embed secret codes in their work. Maybe Twig's earlier works can shed some light on where he hid his final manuscript."

Nix Arssen glanced down sadly. "Mr. Cage's recent films have little value, I fear. It is a case of a once-promising career derailed by a series of degrading roles. Frankly, I feel you are scraping the bottom of the herring barrel."

"Perhaps. But it's worth a try. You never know."

"Any success finding the manuscript?"

"Not yet, *Meister.*"

"How many fingers, Reinhard?"

"*Eins, zwei, drei, vier, fünf* . . . five and a half, master."

Dagher Ukea sucked on a golf-ball-sized rock of crystal meth. He switched off the speakerphone and spoke quietly into the receiver. "Listen, Reinhard. I'd like to meet with you in person. Have a little face-to-face chat."

"*Jawohl,* master. Reinhard come to your office right away."

"*No!* No need for you to do all that driving, Reinhard. Let's meet outside the city. I could use a little fresh air and you deserve a break from all that reindeer strangling. I know this nice quiet spot that UKEA has used in the past as a mass grave. There we won't be disturbed. We can have a nice chat in private. Maybe we can even take a walk. Let's meet in an hour. That should leave us with plenty of daylight, right?"

"*Jawohl,* master. Trolls no come out until four-fifty today."

"Great. I'll see you in a bit."

Blomberg returned to Salamander's cell with Arssen's three manuscripts. There he was joined by Chief Inspector Bubbles. They each took one manuscript.

"Fuck, this is long," said Lizzy. She flipped to the back—557 pages, in Cambria 12 point. She hadn't read a novel since *Vilfred Come Home* in third grade. Frankly, she wasn't sure if she could. Relativistic space cosmology, heterotic-E string theory was one thing—but an unpublished novel?

"Maybe you guys should count me out of this one," she said.

"You don't have to read for content," said Blomberg. "You're looking for patterns, codes, encryptions. All right up your alley."

"Okay. But I'm going to need *a lot* of Twinkies."

Blomberg sucked pre-Columbian espresso from a CamelBak while Bubbles sipped mint tea. They read in silence.

Every couple of minutes, however, Salamander checked her iPhone and did some light kickboxing.

After an hour or so, Blomberg caught her gaming. "C'mon, Lizzy. Focus."

"Fuck you, Kalle. I hate reading this shit. I have learning disabilities as a result of my upbringing. You try being shot in the brain."

"Try turning off your iPhone."

"You turn off your fucking iPhone."

"I did."

Salamander impatiently broke open a fresh box of strawberry-filled Twinkies. "Fucking plastic wrap drives me crazy."

"Maybe all that sugar isn't good," said Blomberg.

"I've told her that before," said Bubbles.

"Why don't you assmunchers mind your own business? Don't you also have reading to do?" To her alarm she noticed that they had read twice as much as she had. *How do they read so fast? They must skim.*

She discreetly removed her tongue stud and jammed it into her palm. *That should help me focus.*

"Lizzy, your hand is bleeding."

"Mind your own fucking business."

They read all through the day. For dinner they ordered pizza delivery from Big Bill's.

"Is pepperoni and extra cheese okay with you guys?" Salamander asked.

"I don't eat pork," said Bubbles.

"Could we have a half of fried eel?" asked Blomberg.

They got two pies—one extra cheese; the other, half pepperoni, half fried eel—and a couple of liters of Thorkill's Root Beer.

Blomberg and Bubbles finished first. Together they watched a couple of episodes of CSI Norrbottens Iän on Salamander's 50-inch B&O flatscreen. They kept it on mute so as not disturb Salamander. She finished shortly before midnight.

"So what do we have?" asked Bubbles.

"Fifteen hundred pages of dreck," suggested Salamander.

"Let's report one at a time," said the inspector.

Blomberg went first. "Where should I begin? The manuscript is a total mess. It's one of those typical British boarding-school stories. The protagonist is an orphan. He lives with his aunt and uncle who treat him shabbily and make him sleep in a cupboard. Then he gets a scholarship to go off to this very posh boarding school and becomes a real hero. Only it's not a normal boarding school. It's a school for little wizards, and I don't mean academically gifted children. It turns out that the kid has magic powers."

Bubbles and Salamander groaned.

"I know—completely implausible. And it gets worse. The kid spends his days playing soccer on a broomstick and learning how to cast spells and make potions. And this goes on for *hundreds* of pages. The strangest thing is that it appears that Twig really thought this crap could sell. There's a note that he wrote to himself on the title page describing how he'd spend all the millions the book would earn."

"Poor guy."

"Anything about reindeer?" Salamander asked.

"Nothing. Just about every animal under the sun appears, though. There are several owls, a rat that turns into a wizard, a werewolf, a three-headed dog, some flying monstrosity that turns out to be a cross between a griffin and a mare. But no reindeer."

"Anything else that might be a clue?"

"I don't think so. The kid has a tattoo on his forehead in the shape of a lightning bolt, which made me think of the double lightning bolt, the symbol of the SS. I thought the kid was going to turn out to be a neo-Nazi, but lo and behold, the mark is just a scar is from a childhood injury."

"Anything else?'

"A dark wizard who's trying to destroy the world, but he seems to be patterned more after Pol Pot or Saddam Hussein than Hitler. That's about it."

"The manuscript I read is, if possible, even worse," said Bubbles. "It's about this American professor of symbology at Harvard—"

"Does Harvard even have a chair in symbology?" asked Blomberg.

"Sounds pretty ridiculous, doesn't it? But maybe the professor trained at that English boarding school for wizards."

All three laughed.

"In any case, this *world-famous* Harvard symbology professor is asked to help solve the murder of a curator at the Louvre whose body has been left naked and pinned to the floor in the pose of the Vitruvian Man."

"Off to a plausible start," said Blomberg.

"I always loved that Leonardo," said Salamander. "My father got me a poster of it when he was in Italy on business, assassinating a NATO general. It hung on the wall in my bedroom."

"Didn't Bill Gates buy the original?"

"That was the Codex Leicester," corrected Salamander. "Vitruvian Man is in Venice."

Bubbles continued. "The manuscript is filled with ridiculous codes and encryptions, all incredibly primitive. There's a secret Swiss bank account numbered 1 1 2 3 5 8 13 21."

Salamander laughed derisively.

Blomberg didn't get it.

"Fibonacci numbers," she explained. "A code for three-year-olds. A code for Nicolas Cage movies."

Odd that his name should come up again, thought Blomberg. He remained baffled. Math had not been Blomberg's strong suit.

"I'll explain later," said Salamander.

"There's a lot of stuff about the Vatican," said Bubbles, "and about secret Jesuit organizations and about the Holy Grail and Jesus Christ. But nothing about Hitler and reindeer. And it goes on for hundreds and hundreds of pages."

"How is the prose?"

"Wooden. The characters are flat, a collection of tics and idiosyncrasies. There's no attention to psychology and motive."

"Sounds truly awful," said Blomberg. "Even back in journalism school we knew that Twig was a dreadful writer, but I never knew just how bad he really was. It's almost beyond belief."

"What's so strange is that he seemed to think this manuscript would also sell. He wrote on the title page: 'Advance will go to down payment on a villa on Mallorca.'"

"Maybe Chamelea did him a favor decapitating him."

"Okay, Lizzy, how about your manuscript?"

"Well, this one is also a real mess. It's about . . . I'm not even really sure where to start . . ."

Brow furrowed, Salamander flipped nervously through a couple of pages of sloppy notes she'd quickly scribbled. Bubbles and Blomberg glanced at each other. They were used to seeing her aggressively in control of all situations.

"Why don't you start by telling us about the main character?"

"That's just it. There are so many fucking different characters and they all have ridiculous names. They're all searching for this woman named Five."

"Five?"

"Yeah, and I'm not even really sure if Five exists. She seems to change from chapter to chapter."

"Is she a wizard?"

"I dunno. The book goes all the fuck over the place. First these navy guys are chasing alligators in the New York sewer system. Then the book jumps back in time to Egypt. It's all a mess."

Blomberg and Bubbles gave each other another look.

"Hey, you guys try reading this fuckpile if you don't believe me."

"Any reindeer?"

"Not that I noticed. Just those alligators in the New York sewer system."

"So what are we left with?"

"Nothing."

"What if we take all the letters from the first word of every chapter?" asked Bubbles. "Maybe that will tell us something about reindeer or the missing manuscript."

"Tried that," said Salamander. "I got SNICKERIFABRIK-SWEDISHMAKESMELAUGH. Not too promising."

"Did you run a DES?"

"Data encryption standard," Salamander explained to Blomberg. "Like, duh. Nothing."

"Maybe he was using a Feistel function."

"Checked that. Nope."

"Symmetric key algorithm?"

"Negative."

"Skipjack cipher?"

"No, siree."

"There must be *something*."

They sat around nibbling on cold pizza crust. Blomberg picked the pieces of fried eel off a leftover slice and ate them. Salamander shadow-boxed.

"Didn't you say he kept a blog?" she asked, delivering a death blow to an imaginary forehead.

"His father said no one read it, not even Twig."

"Well, I saw this Nicolas Cage movie where the character hides a secret message in his blog. It's worth a shot."

The girl parked her Saab 9-3 FWD by a stand of birch trees at the far end of the field. She had stopped twice during the three-hour drive, once to repair the clutch and a second time to reconstruct the engine mount. Tracking the monstrous freak had been a piece of cake. The moron had registered his Palm Treo Pro under his own name. All she had to do was hack into the smartphone and follow the GPS. Even her stupid fucking twin sister could have done it. Who fancied herself such a prime-time hackstar. Well, welcome to the big time, kiddo. In fact, the giant had made things so simple that at first she suspected a trap, but now she'd come to realize that he was just a hopeless douche. And a weirdo. He moved only during the day and appeared never to go any-where at night. What kind of assassin was he, anyway? As far as she could tell, he'd never killed a soul. Just a bunch of fucking reindeer.

Too bad. He still had to die. He never should have accepted a contract on her head. And he never should have destroyed that Brio Santa's sleigh. *Sorry, you big goon.*

She lay on the frozen ground and peered through her Leica Geovid 15×56 HD 56 BRF Binoculars with Laser Rangefinder. There he was in the same outlandish shearling coat his twin brother used to wear. It was hard to believe that she and the freak shared a quarter of the same genes. *Father was only about six feet. Their mother must have been a fucking amazon. Those East Germans grew their women BIG.*

He wore no hat or gloves. It must have been around −35 degrees. He hadn't even bothered to button his coat. *Boy's going to catch cold if he's not careful.*

She'd stolen the binoculars from a commander of a special operations helicopter unit of the Swedish navy. *Sick optics.* She examined the giant's fingers. *Poor dumb fuck. Gotta mind those digits if you're going to pack a shank.*

She patted her Thaitsuki Nihonto Katana sword made from high carbon Japanese steel. Maybe she'd take a thumb as a souvenir.

She'd been watching for several minutes when an antique convertible blue Mercedes 770K pulled up to a stop beside the giant. Out stepped Dagher Ukea. *Whoa. Dickhead doesn't even drive a Swedish car. Well, prepare to die. Two for the price of one.*

Ukea and the giant shook hands. Then they disappeared into an abandoned warehouse at the far end of the field. Distance 437 meters, said the laser rangefinder. A cinch using a Bravo 51 with telescopic sight. Only she preferred to work up close.

She wrapped a kaffiyeh scarf around her head in the manner of the mujahideen. Then she stripped down to her girl ninja outfit. Wearing the rubber-soled ninja slippers that she'd bought at H&M, she silently moved across the frozen field. In the distance she saw a reindeer. *I'll deal with you later.*

From the warehouse came the sound of a small explosion. Instinctively she flung herself on the ground. She waited for her heart to stop pounding before she got up and ran across the field. She had to walk halfway around the warehouse to find an open door. But no sooner had she slipped inside than she heard the sound of a car driving off. *Fuck, there goes Ukea. Will have to decapitate him another day.*

She continued searching for the giant. She found him in a big room with broken windows and stacks of rotten pallets. Thick furniture bolts stuck out from either side of his neck, spurting blood with every heartbeat. Moving closer, she saw that the giant's hands and feet had been nailed to the floor, making him into a table.

She stood over him, peering down.

"You still alive?"

"Yes."

"Who did this to you?"

"*Der Meister.*"

"Who's the master?"

"Herr Ukea."

"Hold on a sec. Don't die just yet."

From her ninja fanny pack the girl removed her Flip mino HD video camera.

"Would you mind repeating that," she said. "Who killed you?"

"Herr Ukea."

"The Ukea family is pretty big. Which Herr Ukea?"

"Dagher Ukea."

"How did he kill you?"

"He nail me."

"With a gun?"

"Automatic nail gun. He laugh. Now Reinhard am at his end. Reinhard am end table."

Sick fuck, that Dagher.

"Why did Ukea kill you?"

"Not happy with Reinhard's work."

"What work?"

"Assassin work."

"Who were you supposed to assassinate?"

"Lots of person. You. Other half sister Lizzy. Fat journalist Blomquvist."

"Berg."

"Yes."

"Why did Ukea want you to assassinate all these people?"

"Looking for book. By bad unpublished writer. Who you decapitate."

"Hold, on a sec. Let's just re-record that last bit."

The girl shot some video of the warehouse for atmospherics and then put away her Flip.

"Are you in pain?"

"What is pain?"

Right. Forgot about that.

"Half sister Chamelea?"

"Yes, Reinhard."

"Please don't leave Reinhard for the trolls."

"The trolls?"

"Yes. Trolls come at night."

"Okay, Reinhard. I'll stay with you, I promise." From her fanny pack she removed a book. "I have the newest by Henning Mankell. Would you like me to read it to you?"

"Reinhard no like Mankell. But, yes. Read. Please."

She had read a couple of pages when she noticed little steam clouds were no longer emerging from the giant's mouth. He was gone.

Salamander powered up her Tera 10 mainframe, causing a small brownout in the nearby township of Tyresö. After a couple of seconds of searching it was clear that Twig's blog had been deleted from the web and replaced by a stub. No huge surprise there. Just showed that someone didn't want others reading the blog. Of course, that in itself was of some relevance. Why bother removing a blog that no one was paying any attention to in the first place? The effort suggested something there *worth* deleting.

Of course, you had to feel for the moron who thought that removing the blog from the web and deleting it from search engines would actually expunge it from cyberspace. It was still there *somewhere*. Some loser in Iceland, some asswipe in Estonia, some freak in Finland had no doubt read the blog, then downloaded it and posted it and sent it to a friend. It was just a matter of finding that someone.

It took seven minutes. *Longer than I would have thought.* A genetics student at Linnaeus University maintained a webpage devoted to Contemporary Swedish Dadaism. Under the heading "Wordsmiths of the Web," the student had written:

Here's a small body of recent poems, weird one-line creations that remind me of haiku playing hanky-panky with Dada. I found them on the blog of a writer who uses the nom de plume *Angst Wiser*. Got to love it! Read and enjoy!

The name immediately caught Salamander's attention. *Angst Wiser? Twig Arssen, puh-leeze. Not the anagram game.*

There were four cryptic one-line poems beneath a cryptic title:

FOUR DADAIST POEMS
(DEDICATED TO A CLUELESS JERK)

1. ED HEROINE TREK LION

2. A BRIGHT CHEW KIT

3. A CAD WHETHER ME NIGHT STINK

4. A CREEPED HORN SLUT

Salamander shook her head dismissively. *Dada poetry? I don't think so.* Why couldn't people playing with secret codes ever give her *real* challenges?

She sent a text to both Bubble and Blomberg.

<figured out the reindeer thing. even KFB could have solved this one.>

"We have one less psychopathic assassin to worry about." Officer Snorkkle brought Bubbles the news. "This morning we got an anonymous tip to go to an abandoned warehouse north of the city. And guess who we found there?"

"Who?"

"C'mon, guess."

"Officer, I'm *not* in the mood."

Hasn't he gotten awfully touchy since he started carrying on with Lizzy?

"Reinhard Niemand, sir. He'd been nailed to the floor. Made into an end table."

"Something new for UKEA's spring catalog. Suspects?"

"The usual. Chamelea Salamander. Dagher Ukea. No one else comes to mind."

"Evidence?"

"We found a copy of the newest book by Henning Mankell near the body. We dusted it for prints. Nothing."

"A killer with literary tastes."

Snorkkle cleared his throat. "With all due respect, sir, I wouldn't exactly call Henning Mankell literature."

"He hid the manuscript in a reindeer with a large rack and white chest markings that lives near the famous old spruce in Dalarna."

"You've got to kidding," said Blomberg.

"I wish I were."

Salamander showed Blomberg and Bubbles the simple anagrams.

ED HEROINE TREK LION = Look in the reindeer

A BRIGHT CHEW KIT = With the big rack

A CAD WHETHER ME NIGHT STINK = And the white chest marking

A CREEPED HORN SLUT = Near the old spruce

"Who do you think the message was intended for?"

"My guess would be Jerker Ekkrot. The blogs were written shortly before Ekkrot was murdered."

"Maybe that's why Ekkrot was killed first. To stop him from getting to the manuscript."

"It's possible," said Bubbles. "Though I still don't understand why Chamelea had to murder them if all she wants is proof of the connection to Hitler. I can understand why Ukea would want Twig dead. And if Ekkrot had directions to publish if anything happened to Twig, then I can understand why Ukea would target him, too. But Chamelea? It's as if she were doing Ukea a favor. Why wouldn't she just let Twig publish?"

Salamander shrugged. "Sis is one fucked-up chick."

"But so fucked up as to kill without reason?"

"Can we step back a moment," said Blomberg. "How exactly does one hide a manuscript *in a reindeer*? Am I alone in finding that odd?"

Salamander cracked open a topology textbook. She didn't like all the parsing. Math made sense, not people.

"Odd," said Bubbles. "But not unheard of. In the early 1980s, the Latvians inserted nuclear secrets in an elk."

"You mean, some guy sedated an elk, made an incision, planted nuclear secrets in its belly, and stitched it up?"

"The history of Baltic espionage is filled with such stories."

"So what went wrong? You're telling me that Niemand decoded

the blog? I doubt Niemand could spell reindeer if you spotted him all the consonants."

"Not Niemand. Probably Ukea. He then hired Niemand."

"I thought we said Ukea just killed Niemand."

"Maybe he didn't like Niemand's habits of leaving digits at crimes scenes. Maybe he panicked, thinking the trail would lead back to him."

"Why strangle the reindeer? Why not just shoot them and cut them open?"

"Niemand obviously wanted to throw us off the trail by making us think we were dealing with a Reindeer Ripper. In this, I have to say, he was quite successful."

"And now Chamelea has joined the act?"

"She must have also found the blog. That or she realized what Niemand was doing and figured out the logic to his killing."

"Where does that leave us? Are we now supposed to go around slaughtering every reindeer that happens to live near an old tree?"

"Not just any tree. The Dalarna spruce is the oldest tree in the entire world."

"That's not the point. The whole thing's ridiculous. There must be thousands of reindeer with big racks and white chest markings that live near that spruce."

"Perhaps. I'll check with Svenssen over in Reindeer at the Institute."

"Forget about Svenssen. The whole thing makes *no* sense. Did Twig expect Ekkrot to go around butchering reindeer that fit his description until he finally found the right one?"

"It *does* seem inefficient."

"It seems *insane.* Something's not right."

The girl smiled at the bouncer by the entrance to Klub Kharma, a dance club popular with the Valhallavägen hip-hop scene. She had recently dyed her hair blond, her natural color: the black had been a bitch to get out. She wore a stop-sign-red miniskirt. In her stiletto heels she barely broke five feet. She balanced an aquavit on her head while dancing to DJSving.

A drunken Östermalmstorg litigator drew close. "Slut wanna suck my mulkku?"

The girl reached over and tore the guy's ear off, then shouted in the ear, "I think I'll pass." She tossed the ear on the floor.

This created something of a commotion.

A tough biker gal from Kungälv approached her. "Ballsy. C'mon, let's dance."

Which they did.

"Love your tattoo," the biker said. "Is that a Siberian sturgeon?"

"Baltic."

"Cool. Where'd you learn to do that sick spin move while balancing the aquavit on your head?"

"Years of training as an assassin."

"Ha! You want to come back to my place?"

"Maybe another time."

Frankly she would have preferred dancing to the new house bands coming out of Linköping, but the hip-hop gave her a chance to think. She hadn't minded decapitating Ekkrot and Arssen. The sick fucks had it coming to them. But killing random reindeer was something else altogether. That wasn't fun at all. And it made no sense. Who hides a manuscript in an innocent mammal? She was missing something. Ukea obviously didn't have a clue. And who else was there? Twig's father, Nix Arssen, didn't know squat. Otherwise why hire the fat journalist who did nothing but drink coffee and eat fried eel? That left Odder Arssen, Twig's hundred-year-old grandfather, still holed up in Ukea's Asylum for Workplace Injuries and Criminally Insane Employees. She'd met Odder several times during her own year at the asylum and had liked the old man, who, out of respect for her presumed ancestry, always greeted her with a stiff-armed salute and a crisp *Heil!* But even then Odder had been too far gone to answer any of her questions, and had just spent his days lying on the bed of his squalid 76-square-foot room, propped up against his five decade-of-service pillows. According to the nursing staff, UKEA kept sending him a new pillow every ten years, the same hideous reindeer-motif—

The girl froze in the middle Fattaru's number-one single, "Fatta eld." The bottle of aquavit slid off her head and crashed to the floor. She raced over to her purse and grabbed her General Dynamics Sectéra Edge SME PED smartphone. It took her two minutes to hack into the database of the UKEA Asylum for Workplace Injuries and Criminally Insane Employees. From the central menu she accessed the visitors' log. Two weeks before his duly deserved decapitation, Twig had visited his grandfather, his first visit in over ten years.

Bingo!

It was one of the few games from America that she enjoyed. That and Clue.

<u okay?>

The text message arrived at 2:17 AM. It was from Mia Hu, Salamander's kickboxer friend and erstwhile fuckbuddy. Not that Salamander was a lesbian. Of *course* not.

Salamander hadn't heard from Hu in six months. Their friendship had never entirely recovered from the time a couple of years back when Salamander had let Hu stay in her apartment but had forgotten to tell her that she was being pursued by a team of international assassins. Fortunately Hu didn't hold grudges and the prosthetic legs still permitted her to kickbox.

<any reason why I shouldn't be?>
<the way u dropped that bottle of aquavit & tore out of the club.>

Salamander closed her book on Riemannian geometry and sat up.

<u say i tore out?>
<how would u put it?>
<i spose . . . >
<tho i love the blond look & the red miniskirt. a whole new lizzy>
<u cld say that>
<i followed u but I guess u didn't see me. i saw the fresh
 wheels. when did u get the 93? i thought u hated saabs>
<change of spirit. did u like the color?>
<would have preferred black>
<to what?>
<huh?>
<u say you'd prefer black. prefer it to what?>
<the color u got>

<which is what?>

<i think i'm missing something>

Like your brain, you stupid fucking dyke. <what color *is* my car? i'm colorblind, remember?>

<o. not sure i knew. kinda nocturne blue metallic>

Bourgeois color. <thanx>

<want to come over? i got a cool new ratchet screwdriver>

<not 2nite>

<bitch>

<call me that again & i'll have to give u a spanking>

<bitch>

"Could you show me how to download the new Horrible Viking game app to my iPhone?"

"Not now, Pigfuck. Seriously. I'm busy. Come back tomorrow."

"It never takes you more than a second," said Officer Snorkkle.

"I said I'd help you *tomorrow*. Now get the fuck out of my cell."

The officer retreated, head low.

Salamander had to think fast. *Click!* Her sister was in Stockholm. What would be the easiest way to trace her? *Click! Click! The car!* What's the easiest way to trace a Saab? *Click! Click! Click! Through its recall and repair records!*

She hacked into the central database of Saab-Scania AB, then searched the client database by birthday. 12 March 1981. *Two weeks until the big three-O, sis.*

There it was. 2010 Saab 9-3 X turbo. *And, yes, Wu, nocturne blue metallic. Nice call.*

Salamander scanned the recalls:

brake booster; hydraulics system; vacuum hose; fuel pump; ignition discharge module; driver side air bag; front and rear axle; crankshaft; piston rings

Why didn't the ditz buy Japanese? Of course, even Toyota's been taking it on the chin.

The car was registered to one Ursula Undress. *Not all that original, sis. Not to mention Andress is Swiss and now looks like a fucking cow.*

From there things moved quickly. The customer service records listed an email address: u.undress@gmail.com. *So slutty.* That made hacking into Chamelea's computer child's play. *Really too easy to be true.* On her desktop was a folder called "My Recent Hackings." *Clever title. I guess just because you were better than me at baking gingerbread, you thought you could outhack older sis. Well, remember who was born five minutes before whom!*

The folder contained a file called "Arssen." *You're making this sooo hard, Cam.*

And in the file was a document created two hours ago: the record of Twig's recent visit to Odder Arssen.

Bingo!

Not that she'd ever enjoyed the game. Her father had liked to play; somehow Chamelea always won. Lizzy had suspected cheating.

Salamander, Blomberg, and Bubbles piled into the inspector's Volvo XC70 police cruiser. It had snowed another couple of feet overnight and the traffic was light for six in the morning. There was no need for the siren, but Bubbles liked driving with the blue lights flashing.

They'd gone no more than a kilometer when he came to a sudden stop.

"Seat belts!" he commanded.

Lizzy peevishly buckled up.

"Why did Twig visit his grandfather?" asked Blomberg.

"I don't know," said Salamander. "But I know Chamelea thinks it's important. And if I know Chamelea, that's where we'll find her."

"What if it's a trap?"

"You keep assuming that my sister is some master strategist. She's not. She's a fucking skank."

Blomberg nodded. From what he remembered, Chamelea had outperformed Lizzy in every subject in school, except maybe math. But even in math, she'd been pretty good. *No point in pushing this.*

Blomberg called Nix Arssen and told him to meet them at the asylum. Arssen deserved to be on hand for Chamelea's arrest.

They pulled into the visitors' parking lot, which was empty save for a nocturne blue metallic Saab 9-3. It appeared to be leaking oil.

They ran into the lobby. At the reception desk sat a nurse with thin lips and an eye patch. "Visiting hours don't start until ten," she said. "You can spend the next four hours in the waiting room."

"How about the cafeteria?" asked Blomberg.

"That opens at nine."

All at once Salamander head-butted the nurse, knocking her unconscious.

"Fröken Salamander!" shouted the chief inspector.

"Lizzy!" exclaimed Blomberg.

Salamander avoided their angry stares. "Psychiatric hospitals have bad associations."

"Still!" said Bubbles, "If you can't behave, I'll have to arrest you. And believe me, I will."

"*Sorry.*"

Behind the reception area they discovered a second unconscious, head-butted nurse.

"I guess we're not alone."

They found Odder Arssen's room number and hurried to his unit. The padded door to his cell was wide open. But no sooner had they entered than the door slammed shut behind them. They spun around. Before them stood a very petite woman with delicate bone structure and large brown eyes. Blond hair peeked out of her ninja headdress.

"Hey, sis."

"Hello, Cam."

Nix Arssen had beaten them to the asylum. "She's been holding me at knife point," he complained. "My son's murderess."

"Murderer is fine," said Chamelea. "And it's a sword."

Glances were exchanged as each tried to size up the situation. Then all eyes turned to Odder Arssen, who appeared to be sleeping soundly in his narrow cot. Surrounding him were five oversized pillows. The design motif showed a reindeer with a big rack and white chest markings grazing by a spruce.

"Not just any spruce," said Bubbles, as if to himself.

"The Dalarna spruce," whispered Blomberg. "9,550 years old."

Together they absorbed the moment. Only Nix Arssen didn't follow.

"Could someone," he asked, "please fill me in on what's going on?"

"Patience," said Bubbles.

"Who'll do the honors?" asked Blomberg.

"Cam's got the sword," said Salamander. "You promise not to use it on us?"

Chamelea nodded. "For the time being."

Salamander handed her sister the first pillow. Chamelea held her short katana horizontally before her and then gradually drew it over her head. In a flash she'd lacerated a two-millimeter cut through the entire length of the pillow.

Salamander helped her sister remove the stuffing.

"Fiberfill," said Chamelea. "UKEA advertised it as Norwegian duck down."

"It starts with management," said Blomberg.

The first pillow was empty.

As was the second.

And the third.

"I think I have a right to know what's going on," said Arssen. "I fear that when my father awakens and finds his beloved pillows all cut up, he could have a seizure."

"I don't think you have anything to worry about," said Chamelea.

Arssen didn't like her tone. He checked his father's vital signs. These confirmed he was dead.

"I'd say he's been dead at least a day or two," said Chamelea, poised before the fourth pillow.

"The asylum is a disgrace," said Blomberg. "What is this, America?"

Chamelea swung.

Lizzy removed an inch of stuffing before hitting paper. She reached in and pulled out several hundred pages held together by two crisscrossing rubber bands.

"The manuscript," cried Arssen. "What's the title?"

"You can read it for yourself," said Lizzy. "It's all yours."

"Not so fast," said Chamelea. She raised her katana sword and assumed the Messenger of Death position.

Bubbles drew his service revolver. It was his first time in twenty years on the force that he'd ever removed it from its holster. He was dismayed to see it covered with dust.

"Fröken Chamelea Salamander, I order you to drop your weapon. You're under arrest for the murders of Professor Dr. Jerker Ekkrot and Twig Arssen."

Chamelea carefully resheathed her hand-forged sword. "The time it took you to pull your weapon I could have decapitated all of you." Bubbles had to acknowledge there was some truth to her claim. "But you're free to arrest me. Just give me the manuscript."

"And why is that?"

"Because I wrote the book."

TWELVE

ONSDAG, FEBRUARI 23–LÖRDAG, MARS 16

1.d4 Nf6 2. c4 e6 3. Nf3 d5 4. g3 dxc4 5. Bg2 a6 6. Ne5 c5 7.
Na3 cxd4 8. Naxc4 Bc5 9. O-O O-O 10. Bd2 Nd5 11. Rc1
Nd7 12. Nd3 Ba7 13. Ba5 Qe7 14. Qb3 Rb8 15. Qa3!? Qxa3 16.
bxa3 N7f6 17. Nce5 Re8 18. Rc2 b6 19. Bd2 Bb7 20. Rfc1 Rbd8
21. f4!? Bb8 22. a4 a5 23. Nc6 Bxc6 24. Rxc6 h5?! 25. R1c4 Ne3?
26. Bxe3 dxe3 27. Bf3 g6 28. Rxb6 Ba7 29. Rb3 Rd4 30. Rc7
Bb8 31. Rc5 Bd6 32. Rxa5 Rc8 33. Kg2 Rc2 34. a3 Ra2 35.
Nb4 Bxb4 36. axb4 Nd5 37. b5 Raxa4 38. Rxa4 Rxa4 39. Bxd5
exd5 40. b6 Ra8 41. b7 Rb8 42. Kf3 d4 43. Ke4

—GAME 2, SALAMANDER-BUBBLES, 25 FEBRUARI 2010

Chamelea took over Lizzy's cell. Snorkkle couldn't believe his
eyes. "Cunt, Part II," he said. "You are soooo fucked."

Chamelea didn't bother to look up from her Proust. Lizzy had
left everything behind except her Tera 10. She'd even upgraded
the cable package for her B&O 50-inch flat-screen. Only Chamelea didn't watch TV.

Chief Inspector Bubbles arrived the morning after her capture.
"I'd like to ask you some questions."

"Does my sister talk to coppers?"

"No."

"Well, I don't either."

Bubbles reflected on this. "Would you like to play a game of chess?"

"Never learned how."

"You allege to have written the manuscript that we discovered in the possession of Odder Arssen. Do you have any proof of this?"

"Ask my sis."

Bubbles studied her for a moment. "I never got into Proust."

"It picks up after the first thousand pages."

"Maybe I'll try it again one day." He turned to go.

"Hey, copper. In the meantime, you might find this of interest." She tossed him her Flip video camera.

Salamander moved back into her 3,800-square-foot apartment on Svartensgatan. It was nice to be home again, in her vast unfurnished flat. She carried out a stack of moldering Big Bill's pizza boxes and bought a dozen 32-ounce bottles of Coke. That should tide her over for a week or so. She called a moving company and had an eighteen-wheeler deliver her Tera 10 back home.

Rebooting her mainframe she discovered a new document on her desktop. It was from Chamelea. She easily could have sent Lizzy the document by email. Instead, she'd hacked into the Tera 10, something Lizzy would have considered impossible. Salamander was beginning to realize that her sister wasn't quite the twit she made her out to be. In fact, she'd reluctantly concluded that the reason it had been so easy to find Chamelea was because her sister had intended to be found; that she'd gone to Klub Kharma precisely to be seen; and that she'd never really intended to frame Salamander, but in fact had wanted to put Lizzy on her trail. For reasons that Lizzy suspected now were going to become clear.

Salamander opened the file.

Greetings, sis. As one of the world's leading hackstars, you might try a cleverer password than *Walpurgis Night,* which is, after all, our birthday. (Happy 30th in advance!)

And yet some of the most obvious passwords, thought Salamander, *are considered the most secure.*

In any case, my first days in gaol haven't been too bad. I've made peace with Snorkkle by showing him how to download Shazam onto his iPhone. And thanks for leaving your furniture behind. The cross trainer is great. But since when have you been obsessed with Twinkies? Finding all those boxes reminded me how little we know about each other, how we've let the years pull us apart. Not that we were ever bosom buddies. I know you resented me for being Pappa's favorite and for always beating you at Bingo. And I know that life's been hard on you; I can scarcely imagine what it's like to be buried alive. So I feel for you. Honestly.

But life hasn't been a cakewalk for me either, sis. After you set father ablaze—I'm not judging, just stating a fact—I struggled to make sense of it all. I came to realize that we weren't the happy domestic family I'd assumed. I neglected my schoolwork and lost pleasure in skating and frying meatballs. Then I started studying graphic design and felt that at last I had found my direction. I got a job at UKEA and immediately felt at home. I knew that UKEA's founder, Sløber, had led an SS mobile extermination unit during the war, and that his son, Dagher, was an active neo-Nazi. Still, the company offered room for growth and excellent benefits. Also, given that we, or at least I, suspected Hitler to be our grandfather (I know you always insisted on Stalin), who was I to throw stones?

While working at UKEA, I learned of an employee named Odder Arssen. Odder had been locked up in UKEA's asylum ever since he claimed that Hitler created many of the company's early and influential designs. Around this time, I also learned that Dagher had formed a new political party around the slogan "Keep Sweden Safe for Xenophobes." Suddenly I became completely disgusted with the company, whose image had always been so squeaky clean. I filed a lawsuit, hoping to blow the lid off the whole rotten firm. For my efforts I, too, found myself institutionalized. (Just saw our dear Dr. Telepathian on TV4 Fakta, hawking his new memoir.)

After I negotiated my release from the asylum, I hit rock bottom. I had soured on designing napkin rings and had no idea what I wanted to do. I started keeping a journal and joined a writers' group. There, in one of those strange coincidences that life throws our way, I met Twig Arssen. Twig was an unemployed journalist with dreams of literary glory. I told him that I had heard about his grandfather Odder, and it turned out that Twig knew Odder's story about Hitler and the founding of UKEA. Given my own interest in exploring our family's connection to AH, I suggested that Twig and I collaborate on a book about our family histories. We were incredibly excited. We felt certain the book would become a bestseller, win major prizes. And bring down UKEA.

We moved to Berlin to do research. But our research brought us only disappointment. Twig discovered that Hitler had designed very little furniture. What few blueprints he produced were heavy, imposing, and carved with hideous eagles. In the late forties, Odder brought these designs to Sløber Ukea, who prized them because they'd issued from Hitler's pen—but rejected them as out of synch with his new company's lighter aesthetic.

My research into our own family history also led nowhere. From Wehrmacht records, I learned that our grandfather had been—no, not Adolf Hitler, but instead a junior officer injured during the invasion of Silesia. He married a Soviet soldier, our grandmother, while recovering from gonorrhea. After the war, they moved to Moscow, where Father was raised. Any glorious (or inglorious) connection to AH was merely just another of Pappa's bedtime stories.

And so our project on Hitler, ÚKEA, and the two bad grand-pas had unraveled!

At the time Twig and I were crestfallen—Twig especially, as he had pinned all his literary hopes on this book. We moved back to Stockholm and moped. To pull him out of the doldrums, I suggested that we try our hand at a different book, maybe another thriller. I told myself, "Twig's just another one of those talented unpublished writers waiting to catch a break." Then he showed me his earlier manuscripts. I couldn't believe how bad they were. No flair for language, no understanding of character. Unable to focus on one location, he kept jumping around, from English boarding schools to the Vatican, from Egypt to New York sewers.

"This time we're going to write about what we know," I said. "We'll keep our thriller in Stockholm." I helped him with character and plot. Soon I took over the actual task of writing. I found that the writing came effortlessly once I'd gotten a clear picture of my protagonist in mind (guess who I based her on, sis?). I also found that I liked tapping away on the old manual typewriter Twig had bought on eBay. I thought Twig would be grateful for the help, but are Swedish men ever grateful? For gratitude you have to move to Denmark. Twig became defensive, withdrawn, and then, to my astonishment, brutal. He would get drunk, curse my writing, call me a slut and a hack. One night his abuse turned physical.

A week later, we went to dinner at the house of his friend Jerker Ekkrot, the expert on Baltic sturgeon. I was excited to meet him. Even as a little girl (this must come as a surprise to you), I loved the Baltic sturgeon more than any other Swedish fish, and always looked forward to our lessons on sturgeon at school. (Hence the tattoo.) But as soon as I met Ekkrot I knew he was a bastard. When I praised his book, he laughed cynically as if he'd heard it all before. During the meal, he and Twig ignored me and got terribly drunk. Then they dragged me down to Ekkrot's cellar. Like so many Swedish men, he had converted it into a dungeon of torture and sexual sadism. They proceeded to do unspeakable things to me. Things I never knew could be done with whips, molten wax, and hamsters.

Did I run away? No. Why? I don't think I need to explain to you, of all people, the complex reasons that keep a woman in subjugation. We both saw what Mother endured, though only you understood. But I did go to Twig's father. I begged him to talk to his son. He called his son an underachiever but otherwise refused to acknowledge a problem.

In the meantime, Twig had begun to realize that my book

was pretty good (never, of course, praising me to my face). He would lock me in a room with my typewriter and let me out only after I'd produced two thousand words.

This went on for months. When I finally finished, he took the manuscript, crossed my name off the title page, and threw me out of his apartment. I came back several hours later to find that he'd changed the locks. I didn't know what to do. So I returned to Berlin, stayed with friends, and took up martial arts training again. Then one day I read his blog, and that's when I decided to come back to Stockholm.

———

"I finished reading the manuscript," said Blomberg. He handed the sheaf of papers back to Nix Arssen. "Thank you for letting me read it."

"You're very welcome. It's the very least I could do, seeing that you discovered it."

They were sitting in Angstrom's Literaturklub, popular with the editors at Norstedts Förlag.

"So nothing about UKEA and furniture design and Hitler," said Blomberg. "It was all a red herring."

"Yes, so to speak. Twig must have changed his mind."

"It's all rather ironic. We all were working from a false assumption. In Dagher Ukea's case, with dire consequences. I'm sure you've heard that he's been indicted for the murder of Reinhard Niemand."

"From what I understand, he also contracted Niemand to kill several other persons. Including you."

"Well, I suspect I won't have to worry about Dagher Ukea for some time to come. He could get six years."

"Perhaps seven. Courts have gotten tough with killers in recent years."

Blomberg sipped from his bucket of Eyjafjallajökull dark brew. "I must admit, I wasn't expecting a novel."

"Fiction was always Twig's first love."

"Yes. I read his earlier manuscripts. This one is quite different."

"I suppose."

"He finally set a thriller in Stockholm."

"Write what what you know," said Arssen, smiling thinly. He hadn't touched his Perrier.

"Well, I really was quite impressed. This book's excellent."

"I agree."

"Tighter sentences. Sharper, more rounded characters. Better plot."

"Obviously my son improved over time."

"Improved remarkably, I'd say. Not a flattering picture of our city, though. I never knew Twig was so interested in violence against women."

"Well, of course, he was always a sensitive person."

"Interesting, too, that he'd choose to base his central character on Lizzy Salamander. Without ever having met her."

Arssen moved the bottle of Perrier several centimeters to the side. "Fröken Salamander has been in the news on many occasions over the years, Mr. Blomberg."

"All those details about her childhood. Did he get those from the news, too?"

"What are you trying to suggest, Mr. Blomberg? Not that it's of any great concern to me. You found the manuscript. I've paid you more than adequately. Now you can go back to your blog."

"Then we're on the same page, Mr. Arssen. I was thinking about writing my next blog on the topic of ghostwriters."

Arssen's eyes narrowed. "Unfortunately Chamelea Salamander is not a ghost, Mr. Blomberg. She's all too real. All too real and all too disturbed."

"You give her story no credence?"

"First she claims that Hitler was her grandfather, next that she's the author of Twig's book. Where do the lies stop? May I remind you that she was institutionalized."

"She was also Twig's girlfriend. For three years."

"I believe it was closer to two."

"And yet you never mentioned this during our discussions."

"An honest omission."

"You use that phrase a lot: 'an honest omission.'"

Nix Arssen dabbed at his lips with a napkin though he'd had nothing to eat or drink. "I'm a busy man, Mr. Blomberg. You'll have to excuse me."

"I thought you were long retired."

"I have an afternoon of meetings with agents and publishers, all interested in my son's book."

Lizzy examined the various dummy accounts and illegal holdings. Like most corporate thieves, Dagher Ukea was a complete moron when it came to protecting his personal data. But the man had chutzpah, no denying that. By her reckoning he'd siphoned off nearly 3.2 billion kronor from UKEA to his various offshore personal accounts. How he'd managed not to be caught was beyond her. Didn't UKEA have accountants? *They must have used an American firm.*

Now it was time to redistribute that wealth. Ukea wasn't going to need it; he was going to prison for six, maybe seven years. In principle, it all should have been returned to the company, but principles only went so far when it came to dealing with multinational monstrosities. She transferred 3 billion back to the company's pension fund. That left her a 200,000,000-kronor commission.

Using a software program that she herself had written, Salamander set up four dummy accounts under different aliases. Each account was assigned to a separate shell corporation. The invoices for each company were covered by credit cards that interlocked. Deposits into these accounts were automatically smurfed into smaller packages that were filtered through accounts that Salamander had set up several years earlier to plunder billions from another psychopath of global capital. These deposits were then again randomly redivided and transferred back and forth between Salamander's various shell corporations at lightning speed until the transactions were untraceable. Salamander smiled at her own ingenuity but also mouthed a prayer of thanks for the banking systems of Belize, Cyprus, Malta, and Panama.

Spending the loot was the next order of business. Houses in Greenland were remarkably affordable. She knew it was Bubbles's dream to have a cozy Arctic bungalow. Why she wanted to buy him one wasn't clear to her. Was it a gift for having taught her how to almost trust a man? Or was it a means of now easing him out of her life? Salamander thrust these thoughts from her mind. Introspection was not her strong suit.

She found a dramatic property on sale for €2,600,000. The price was affordable, but did Bubbles really need 93,000 square miles? It seemed . . . excessive.

Then she found an attractive house on the outskirts of

Ittoqqortoormiit. Two bedrooms, two bathrooms, library, reno-
vated kitchen, and lovely views of the Arctic Ocean. And it came
with its own sea kayak and herd of musk ox.

Salamander wired the cash from one of her aliases direct to
GrønlandsBANKEN. Then she arranged to purchase the house
from her alias, so the deed would appear in her name. This she
would sign over to Bubbles.

Ukea's mansion on the Cayman Islands would make a nice
gift for her sister—something to look forward to for when she got
out of prison. As for Ukea's Dassault Falcon 50EX corporate jet,
that she transferred to KFB. Not that she expected Blomberg to
use it. She just wanted to see his face.

She considered giving Ukea's Ferrari Enzo to Pigfuck, but decided against it. He could barely manage his iPhone.

For herself she took Ukea's flotilla of decommissioned war-
ships. Salamander had always wanted her own Destroyer.

She powered down her Tera 10. It was a morning well spent.
But her work was not quite over.

Nix Arssen returned to his 1,208-square-foot apartment in Vasa-
staden after another long day of meetings with agents and publishers. Frankly he was surprised by the amount of interest the
manuscript was generating. Agents wooed him with lunches of
dill-cured salmon, and publishers spoke of pan-Scandinavian book
tours, international rights, and even the possibility of a Brio tie-in.
It was all a bit exhausting.

He turned on the light to the living room and was startled to
find Lizzy Salamander sitting in his Danish Stressless chair.

"I see criminality runs in the family," he said. "I believe this is called breaking and entering."

Salamander nibbled on a Twinkie and let the wrapper drop to the floor.

Such ill-breeding!

"What can I do for you, Fröken Salamander? I suggest you answer me, as I'm about to call the police."

"My sister wrote that book. And you know it."

"Your sister decapitated my son."

"Your son gang-raped my sister. And stole her intellectual property."

"Then go to court, Fröken Salamander," said Arssen. "It might surprise you to hear this, but our nation does have a legal system. It's the same system that's about to try your sister for double homicide."

Salamander shook her head. "I don't believe in courts. I believe in self-help."

"Meaning?"

"That I'll flay your fucking face unless you give me my sister's manuscript." She brandished Chamelea's katana ninja sword. Chamelea had given it to her for safekeeping.

"You're as sick as your sister, the murderess."

"Gender-specific nouns went out with the Volvo 240, you dickhead. And murderer or not, she's a fucking incredible writer. Now give me that manuscript."

From a desk drawer Arssen removed a sheaf of papers and handed it to Salamander. "There. In its entirety. Now leave my apartment this instant."

Salamander calmly riffled through the manuscript, then rose to leave.

Arssen watched her open the front door and step into the hallway. "You sick bitch," he said. "You think I haven't made multiple copies? I'll see you in court."

"I can't accept this gift," said Chief Inspector Bubbles. He examined the deed made out by the GrønlandsBANKEN.

"Don't consider it a gift, then," said Salamander. "Consider it a . . . *something*."

They sat in Brunö's, a new kaffeklub popular with the Siktuna real estate brokers.

"How could you possibly afford this?"

"I invested early in Apple."

Bubbles studied her closely. "You understand that I can't possibly accept this if the money used to purchase was acquired illicitly."

"I swear on my father's grave it's all aboveboard."

Bubbles fingered the deed. "It really is extraordinarily generous of you."

"I also signed you up for a beginner's course in Greenlandic. It's one of the few languages whose morphosyntactic alignment is ergative."

Bubbles smiled. "You're sure you won't come with me?"

"A country without people—it is tempting. But no."

"What will you do?"

She shrugged. "Herd reindeer, I suppose."

"Seriously?"

"No. Chamelea and I are thinking of collaborating on a book. Not that I can write my way out of fishbowl. We've also talked about opening a school for girl ninja."

"She'll be out of prison in less than two years."

"Blomberg's sister is a good advokat."

"And now Chamelea also has a huge advance."

"Which she had to share with that fuckwad Arssen."

"It was a Solomonic decision."

"It was a fucked-up decision. Twig didn't write a word."

"She couldn't prove that."

"We'll see what the appeals court says."

Salamander insisted in picking up the tab. They left the café and idled on the sidewalk. The day before, the temperature had risen above freezing for the first time since August. Now it was back to −15 degrees. Still, the days were growing longer and it was just a matter of months before the snow would melt and the sun would break through the solid bank of clouds.

Bubbles studied Salamander's face. "You're letting your hair grow in red."

She flashed him a murderous glance. "Don't say it. Don't even *think* it."

"I was just going to say it looks nice. It makes you look more like . . . you."

Salamander looked down, shuffled her feet. She wore black Converse lace-ups. Not everything had changed.

"I also got you a little present," said Bubbles. "For your thirtieth. A bit belatedly."

He handed her a small box wrapped in reindeer-motif paper. Tearing off the paper, Salamander discovered a travel chess set.

"IPhones and iPads have almost killed the travel chess set business," said Bubbles. "But I thought this one was very nice. You can bring it to Ittoqqortoormiit, should you ever visit me."

"Thank you." Salamander smiled shyly, crookedly, confusedly.

"It's the first gift I've ever received that wasn't connected to a fuse."

They exchanged an awkward farewell embrace, almost bumping heads, then kissing quickly on the lips.

"Good-bye, Lizzy."

"Good-bye, copper."

Bubbles watched her walk away, hands thrust in the pockets of her hoodie. She'd taken a dozen rapid steps when he called out, "Hey, fröken, 5199."

"Divides the sum of the cubes of the first 5199 primes." Salamander didn't turn around.

Nanski Plocka, Svenska Fotografers Förbund (SFF)

Before becoming a bestselling thriller author, Lars Arfssen trained members of the Kazakhstani Female Militia in counter-patriarchy maneuvers and worked as a hair stylist in Stockholm's hip Södermalm neighborhood. He studied Old Norse at the University of Uppsala and More Recent Norse in Gotland. In addition to his blockbuster trilogy, Arfssen is best known in his home country for his revisionist history of the Swedish meatball, *En Populär Historien om den Svenska Köttbulle*. He lives in Södermalm with his common-law wife and several children from various relationships.